MUST-DO
WEEKENDS

101 MUST-DO WEEKENDS

Edited by
Renée Lang

RANDOM HOUSE
NEW ZEALAND

A RANDOM HOUSE BOOK published by Random House New Zealand
18 Poland Road, Glenfield, Auckland, New Zealand

For more information about our titles go to www.randomhouse.co.nz

A catalogue record for this book is available from the National Library
of New Zealand

Random House New Zealand is part of the Random House Group
New York London Sydney Auckland Delhi Johannesburg

First published 2009

© 2009 New Zealand Automobile Association,
images as credited page 236

The moral rights of the author have been asserted

ISBN 978 1 86979 286 2

Design: Nick Turzynski, redinc
Printed in China by Everbest Printing Co Ltd

Cover images: front cover, main, Photo New Zealand (Arno Gasteiger),
from l–r, Destination Fiordland (Rob Suisted), Hamilton Regional
Tourism, Stewart Island Experience, Hawke's Bay Incorporated; back
cover, t–b, Destination Marlborough, Destination Northland, Tourism
Central Otago, Destination Northland, Sarah Ell.

Contents

Introduction

The end of a dreary work week brings a weekend full of hope. We have the need for some excitement to lift us up and re-energise us, but too often the weekend becomes filled with routine, packed with the practical but lacking the inspiration.

With the release of our '101 Must Do's for Kiwis' campaign, we found that we had piqued the interest of New Zealanders and their passion for majestic and inspiring places and activities all over the country.

It was time to bring all these thoughts and ideas together into a book to give us all the inspiration to end the working week with the knowledge that an adventure or some excitement is awaiting us.

We are creatures of habit and creatures of routine, but we are better people when we are enthusiastic, when we are interested and when we are animated. That is what travel does. I hope this book will interest and inspire you to do more with your weekends.

Peter Blackwell
Automobile Association

KEY TO CATEGORIES

AA   **ACTIVE ADVENTURES**

E   **EVENTS**

EW   **ECO/WILDERNESS**

FF   **FAMILY FUN**

FW   **FOOD & WINE**

HHC   **HISTORY, HERITAGE & CULTURE**

HT   **HIDDEN TREASURES**

RI   **RELAX & INDULGE**

RT   **ROAD TRIPS**

SS   **SCENIC SPLENDOUR**

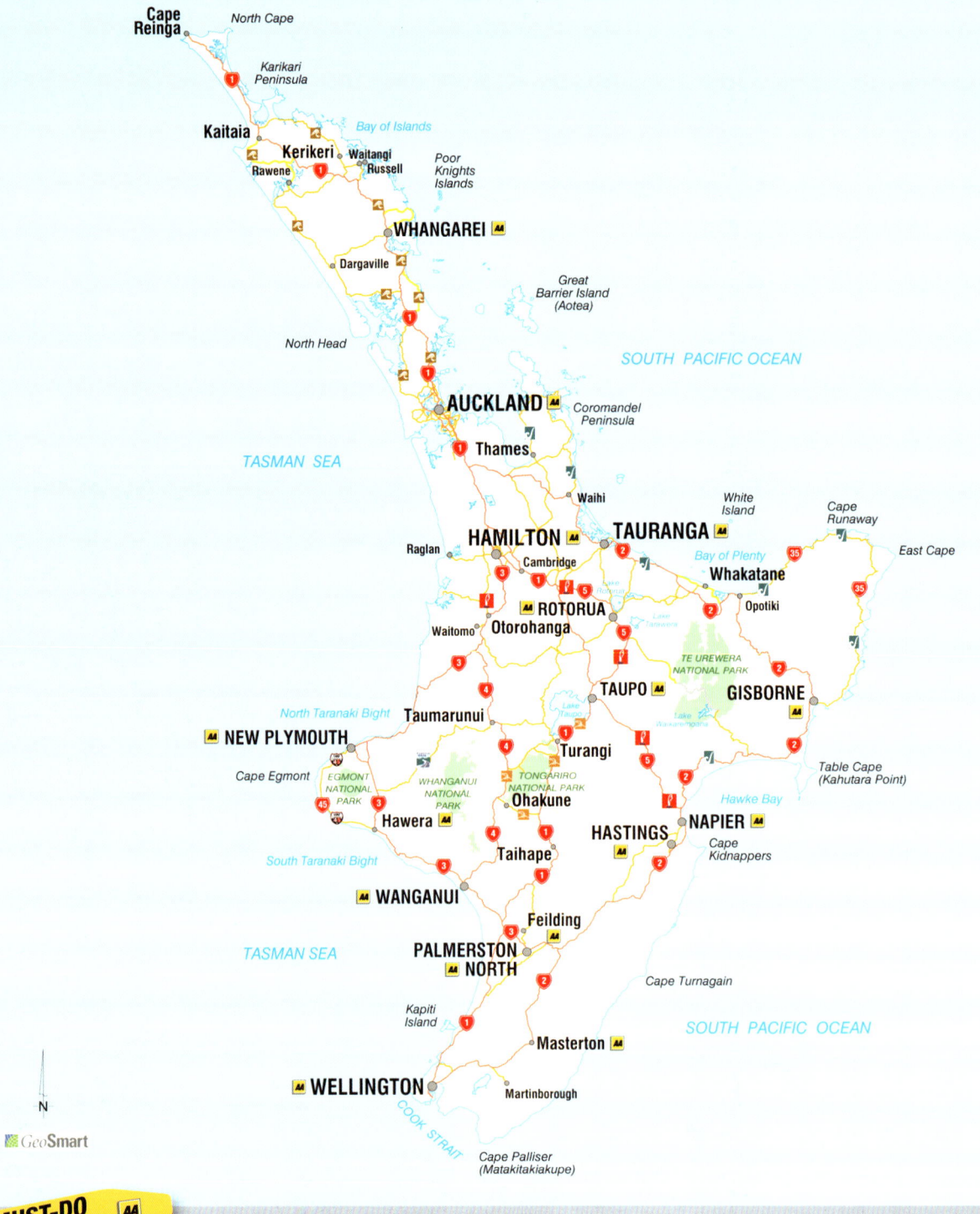

Rotorua Museum

HISTORY, HERITAGE & CULTURE

In the footsteps of Cook

It may well take a bit longer to get to Eastland than many other weekend destinations, but there's no doubt that the extra effort involved pays off. After all, Captain James Cook made it his first port of call back in 1769, so you should put it high on your list, too. Another major claim to fame is Gisborne's status as first city in the world to see the light of each new day.

Your weekend should include a leisurely historic walk through Gisborne City. If it's a Saturday morning, call in to the colourful weekly flea market held in Alfred Cox Park, where you're bound to find various treasures, and if not, then you can stock up on some fresh produce to enjoy over your weekend.

Other highlights of the walk include the city's art deco-style landmark town clock, completed in 1934 as a memorial to a particularly long-serving town clerk; the huge stained-glass window depicting the Tairawhiti district from volcanic origins to the present day, across the back of the HB Williams Memorial Library; and the Tairawhiti Museum (part of which comprises Wyllie Cottage, the oldest European house still standing in Gisborne). Don't overlook a visit to the inner harbour development with its marina, boat-launching ramp and restaurants and cafés. You can say 'hello' to Captain Cook here, or rather to his likeness in the form of a statue, or walk further along the riverbank

The first chunk of New Zealand spotted all those years ago by eagle-eyed Young Nick aboard the *Endeavour*.

and look across to the port, to his original landing place. This is marked by a handsome granite-sheathed concrete obelisk and pedestal that was erected in 1906 and funded through the donation of one penny by every school-age child throughout the country at the time. If possible, soak in the ambience of this special place, now a National Historic Reserve, perhaps over a picnic lunch washed down with some of the region's seriously good chardonnay.

Speaking of wine, you can't visit Eastland without a few cellar-door experiences; after all, it is the country's

Take a walk along Gisborne's mild side; that is, along the riverbank.

You'll see him here, you'll see him there — Captain James Cook is everywhere.

fourth-largest grape-growing region. Most are easily accessible by car from Gisborne —in particular Millton, New Zealand's first certified organic vineyard.

When you're ready for some more exercise, there is no shortage of outdoor activities including horse trekking, guided walks or even a round or two of golf at one of the region's dozen or so golf courses.

13

Birthplace of the nation

The combination of several picturesque villages with a good range of modern facilities and a host of historic sites nearby is too good to miss, so prepare to steep yourself in history up in New Zealand's Far North sooner rather than later.

Base yourself in Russell, Paihia or Kerikeri — none of which is any great distance from each other — and make your first activity a visit to the Waitangi Treaty Grounds, where the Treaty of Waitangi was signed in 1840.

The grounds themselves, with their magnificent lawns, heritage gardens and trees overlooking a Bay of Islands vista, are well worth a visit. But there's lots more to explore including daily tours, cultural activities, workshops such as 'Fun with Flax', and a guided walk that explains the importance of our natural environment and its relationship to Maori society, lore and legend.

Then there is Te Whare Runanga, a fully carved Maori meeting house that's representative of all iwi in New Zealand. On display is *Ngatokimatawhaorua*, one of the world's largest ceremonial war canoes, requiring more than 70 paddlers to get it up to speed. And of course there's the Treaty house itself, built for the first British Resident, James Busby, and his family, and one of New Zealand's oldest and most visited historic homes.

It would be easy to spend the whole weekend in and around the grounds

Not just for decoration; each year this magnificent waka takes part in Waitangi Day commemorations.

because there's so much to see and do. If you feel like stretching your legs take the walking track that links the grounds with Haruru Falls. It's a very pleasant two-hour walk through mangroves and over boardwalks, and when you reach your destination you might enjoy a picnic lunch beside the spectacular horseshoe-shaped cascade falls.

Other physical activities related to the grounds include however many holes you're feeling up to at the Waitangi Golf Course, with its impressive ocean views, or a guided

The Treaty House was originally the home of James Busby, the first British Resident in New Zealand.

kayak tour that will familiarise you with the symbiotic relationship between the region's mangrove forests and coastal ecology.

Wherever you stay in this part of Northland, most of the settlements offer a choice of bars and cafés where you can while away an evening. And in summer a barbecue on the beach featuring local seafood is not a bad option, either.

Maori entertainers and other cultural activities are all part of the Treaty Grounds experience.

Back in the golden days

If you think your local watering hole gets a tad crowded on occasion, spare a thought for what it must have been like towards the end of the nineteenth century in Coromandel's Thames, located on the southern shores of the Hauraki Gulf. Back then it was New Zealand's largest population centre, with 18,000 inhabitants, most of whom were regulars in the town's more than 100 hotels. It's a bit different now that only 7000 people live there. And not surprisingly the number of pubs has dropped accordingly.

The reason for the rise and fall of this — what is by today's standards — small town can be summed up in one word: gold. The precious metal was first discovered in 1867 and led to the establishment of the Shotover Mine, which yielded in its time $845 million worth of gold (at current metal prices).

Waihi went through a similar experience when the Martha vein was discovered in 1878 (the mine is still worked today as an open pit and is the largest known hard-rock mineral deposit in New Zealand).

Today you can try your hand at getting rich quick through official channels, such as at the Goldmine Experience in Thames, where a tour takes you through an operational nineteenth-century stamper battery (an early form of ore crusher consisting of many heavy stamper heads that are raised by water power and fall under gravity into a rotary bowl containing rock to be crushed) and into one of the richest goldmines of the era where you can try your luck at gold panning.

There's also plenty of scope for DIY activity on Rocky's Goldmine Trail, a three-hour walk through regenerating bush with refreshing swimming holes along the way plus vantage points overlooking many gorgeous views.

Further up the road, the town of Waihi promotes itself as having a heart of gold. There are regular tours of the open pit goldmine and the town positively bristles with evidence of its golden past in the form of statues and monuments. And when you want to wash off the gold dust you're not that far from some fabulous beaches.

Nearby you can head off to the Karangahake Gorge where you'll find not only lots of goldmining history, but some beautiful natural surroundings, too. Much of it is accessible through a variety of walks including a former rail tunnel, complete with 'windows', which must have witnessed plenty of comings and goings back when goldmining was in its heyday.

Explore goldmining relics in the Karangahake Gorge.

Waihi's Cornish Pumphouse, built in 1904, was restored and resited in 2006.

Precious pieces of our past

In this age of built-in obsolescence it's rather nice to have a few reminders of the days when things were built to last — and a weekend spent looking for such items to add to your collection can be very rewarding.

There's a clutch of wonderful antique shops that could easily fill up a weekend of browsing in that roughly triangular chunk of the Waikato that takes in Te Aroha, Tirau and Cambridge.

Most have been there for years and are regular ports of call for dyed-in-the-wool collectors. This, of course, has had an effect on prices but 'just looking, thanks' can be lots of fun and you never know when you might come across that special something you can't live without.

If you start in Te Aroha, an attractive little township situated northeast of Morrinsville, there are also some pleasant outdoor options to enjoy including a visit to the historical Te Aroha Hot Springs Domain, where there's plenty to see including the Mokena Geyser. The domain is an easy stroll from the town centre but there are also a number of other local walks varying in length from 20 minutes to 1 hour. Paeroa, about 20 km north, also has some great antique and second-hand shops to rummage about in.

Continue down to Tirau, hard to miss with its dog-shaped information centre smack-bang in the middle of

Straight from the, er, dog's mouth — AKA the information centre for the south Waikato town of Tirau.

town. And that's not the only unusually shaped building — next door to it is a corrugated sheep and there are some very entertaining sculptures including a hunk of cheese, a pukeko, a praying mantis and a cow pushing a shopping trolley. Consider afternoon tea at any of the attractive cafés lining the main thoroughfare before launching yourself at the local antique shops, conveniently open seven days a week, and offering a wide variety of yesterday's treasures.

Then it's on to Cambridge, a thriving

The Cadman Building in the Te Aroha Hot Springs Domain, formerly a bathhouse, is now home to the local museum.

rural town that manages to combine a hint of yesteryear with some very smart shopping and eating options. Again, thanks to the zeal of collectors, the proprietors of the antique shops here are pretty clued up about their stock, so sadly a bargain is unlikely. But you may well get as much pleasure from a relatively inexpensive, dog-eared vintage cookbook as a carved mahogany Victorian wardrobe that would require a second mortgage to purchase . . .

The range of accommodation in any of these provincial towns is plentiful; from basic motel-style units through to luxurious B&Bs.

Deco discovery

It was a good thing the city fathers of Napier decided to rebuild in the art deco style of the day after the horrendous earthquake of 1931 — this architectural style is now responsible for attracting hundreds of thousand of visitors each year.

You can choose to take a guided walking tour of Napier's Art Deco Quarter for a small charge, which will take just a couple of hours, or set out and discover the sights for yourself; but if you're up for a boots'n'all experience, why not enjoy a whole weekend revelling in 1930s style? If the latter appeals, there are two choices. The first takes place each February when the city's Art Deco Trust stages its annual Geon Brebner Print Art Deco Weekend, which attracts a fascinating assortment of classic cars and related miscellany along with lots of people dressed in deco style. Then in July there's the Bluewater Hotel Deco Decanted and Jazz Festival, which provides another opportunity to live the classic lifestyle of the art deco era while enjoying quality jazz from some of New Zealand's best performers.

Napier's sister city of Hastings also has plenty of interesting architecture, much of which was a result of the same earthquake that devastated Napier. Here in Hastings that the Spanish Mission theme prevails; it's an architectural style that originated in California and then spread elsewhere in the New World. Two particularly fine examples are the city's Methodist Church and the Hawke's Bay Opera House and, of course, Westerman's Building, opposite the Hastings Clock Tower, which now houses the Hastings i-SITE visitor centre.

As you'd expect, both cities have generated heaps of informative — and free — brochures that give full details of all the buildings of interest.

In between seeing all of this fabulous architecture, you might want to admire the tasteful and often exquisitely designed buildings associated with the wineries of the region. Hawke's Bay is home to an ever-growing number of players in the wine world, including such revered names as Mission Estate and Craggy Range. And while you're checking out their architecture, it would seem entirely appropriate to sample some of their wares . . .

The New Napier Arch was built to commemorate the city's rebirth after the devastating 1931 earthquake.

If you've got it, flaunt it! Especially if you're heading for Napier's annual art deco weekend.

Experience Maori magic

It's all very well being part of a bicultural society but there are still quite a few of us out there who would really appreciate the opportunity to learn more about Maori culture. Fortunately, a weekend in Rotorua is great for filling in the gaps (did you know, for example, that there are around 35 marae — Maori meeting grounds — in the Rotorua district?). Not only will you come away from a great weekend full of newly acquired knowledge, but there's the chance to have lots of fun in the process.

Be sure to enjoy a hangi or two over the weekend — and perhaps a meal cooked in a geothermal hot spring! Failing that, you're bound to have some good eating experiences in one of Rotorua's many cafés. And when it's time to lay down your head, the accommodation options in the area include a variety of lodges and B&Bs, some with Maori themes.

As in so many other instances, you can take the DIY approach to learning about Maori culture, which ideally involves at least one visit to Rotorua's Te Puia, previously known as the New Zealand Maori Arts & Crafts Institute. Here you can visit their carving and weaving schools, where masters and students share their art and their stories; attend a Maori cultural performance; see significant cultural exhibitions; and enjoy an evening of storytelling, entertainment and Maori kai. There's also the Kiwi House and the Whakarewarewa geothermal valley to explore, both within the korowai (the cloak) of Te Puia. If you'd prefer a guided option, that's no problem, either.

How about combining aspects of Maori culture with a tour of some of the district's highlights? Any number of tour operators offer a blend of cultural activities with trips involving horse trekking, white-water rafting, kayaking or forest trekking, to name just a few. Some tour operators will happily personalise the experience for you or you can join a bigger group — the choice is yours.

And if your aches and pains need attention, consider visiting a Maori healer to experience greenstone meremere healing, Maori herbs, massage or spiritual healing.

Maori art and culture are everywhere you look in Rotorua.

A carver demonstrates his art at the Tamaki Maori Village, Rotorua.

Central heritage

Any time of year is a good time to be in Central Otago. And if you've got an interest in old buildings then there is plenty to look at in the little township of Cromwell, which drew many people to the area in the late nineteenth century when gold was discovered nearby. The construction of the Clyde Dam and subsequent filling of Lake Dunstan in the 1980s brought about some major changes to the town, but the old centre was moved and is now a unique heritage precinct. Wander around the Old Cromwell Town and admire the work that's been done restoring and reconstructing buildings such as the Victoria Arms Hotel, the Masonic Lodge, the old Cobb and Co Store and a wonderful mix of vintage cottages.

Places to visit in and around Cromwell include the Bannockburn Sluicings, the Carrick Goldfield and the Goldfields Mining Centre in the Kawarau Gorge — the mining activity that took place at the height of gold fever has shaped so much of this landscape. As for vineyards, there are too many of them to list here but be sure to track down some local pinot noir and pinot gris, two of the region's exceptionally good wine varieties. During the warmer weather, getting around by bike is a very enjoyable option. Lake Dunstan offers excellent boating and fishing, and for lovers of the great outdoors, opportunities are everywhere for bird watching and enjoying the beautiful public and private gardens featuring many varieties of plants, both indigenous and imported.

Nearby is the well-preserved settlement of Arrowtown, which was founded in 1862 as the result of a gold strike. Like Cromwell, this small township is proud of its heritage buildings and has also made huge restoration and reconstruction efforts that give visitors a pretty good idea of what the place looked like when it was a thriving mining town. For more information on the region's past, a fossick in the Lakes District Museum (considered to be one of New Zealand's best small museums) is highly recommended.

Oh, and if you find yourself anywhere near Cromwell in early December, make sure you stop by the Cherry Spitting Competition. It's been going for several years and it's certainly shaping up to be a fun annual event.

Arrowtown is picturesque in any season, including under snow.

Cromwell's heritage precinct, a safe distance from the waters of Lake Dunstan.

Fall in love with art

In New Zealand's larger centres (and in some smaller ones, too) there are any number of galleries worth visiting where you can view some serious works of art at little or no cost.

At last count there were more than 130 galleries in Auckland alone, a substantial number of which can be found in Parnell, where it's all too easy to spend a whole day wandering between them. From Parnell it's a comfortable commute to the city where, in the area covering Kitchener down to High and Lorne streets, there's enough art to keep you occupied for at least another day, notably Auckland Art Gallery, which houses over 12,500 pieces of art — including works by Maori and Pacific Island artists, as well as European painting, sculpture and print collections.

Wellington has a similarly impressive number of galleries; for instance, the centrally located City Gallery, newly revamped at a cost of $6.3 million, is well worth a visit, and its proximity to Civic Square allows plenty of opportunities for fresh air and caffeine fixes between viewings. It's also not much more than a hop, skip and jump to Te Papa where there's always something to see — you can easily spend a couple of hours in the gift shop alone!

Heading south, there is plenty of artistic scope in and around Nelson (see page 138). Among the better known establishments is

Wellington's sunny Civic Square is home to the City Gallery and Neil Dawson's *Ferns.*

Dunedin Public Art Gallery on the Octagon contains many delights.

the Suter Art Gallery, New Zealand's third-oldest art museum, which regularly hosts a dynamic range of exhibitions.

Moving further south, one of the main jewels in the South Island's gallery crown has to be the Christchurch Art Gallery, which opened in 2003. It's the largest art institution in the South Island and with its two floors of exhibition space, two educational activity areas, an auditorium and a sculpture garden it houses one of New Zealand's most important public art collections. Not far away is the Arts Centre of Christchurch, housed in its distinctive

Gothic Revival buildings where you'll find a great range of New Zealand-made art and crafts, shopping, education and entertainment, including regular festivals.

Both Queenstown and Dunedin also boast a good number of galleries, the latter being home to the long-established Dunedin Public Art Gallery, which in 1996 was relocated to a refurbished building in the heart of Dunedin city.

Akaroa: c'est magnifique!

Given how close the French came to claiming New Zealand as their own back in 1840, we could all be enjoying croissants and café au lait every day, rather than as a special treat. But that was then — and these days the closest you'll get to that special Gallic *je ne sais quoi* is a visit to Akaroa, a historic French and British settlement nestled in the heart of an ancient volcano. It's not much more than an hour's drive from Christchurch, with plenty to see and do on the way. Many of the streets in this charming township have French names, and you won't have to look too hard to find some of the descendants of the original French families still living here.

Much of Akaroa's appeal is that it has something for just about everyone. If you're there for a romantic weekend, well, there are lots of gorgeous places to stay where you can just indulge in the comfort of the accommodation. Or if, say, you're a committed foodie, then you'll probably want to spend all your time checking out the local cafés and restaurants along with some of the artisan food producers in the region. Perhaps you'd prefer to spend as much time as possible out on the water, in which case, no problem! You can charter a boat and go sailing on the harbour or join a cruise on which, if you're lucky, you might spot a rare Hector's dolphin — in any case, examples of varied marine birdlife, seals and penguins are virtually guaranteed. Rather sign up for a fishing charter or go water skiing? Again, all this can be arranged. However, if these options sound too energetic, why not spend your time lazing about on one of the many secluded beaches in one of the neighbouring bays?

Each year Akaroa's French history and heritage are celebrated at the Akaroa Frenchfest, usually held sometime between September and October. Now well established, this event has blossomed into a much anticipated celebration that includes French cooking masterclasses, a special market and a range of outdoor activities (for young and old) that mark Akaroa's unique connections with France.

Crisp blue skies, trendy heritage architecture, energising waterfront walks — Akaroa's got it all.

Café is of course a French word, so where better to enjoy *une tasse*?

The mighty kauri

Can you begin to imagine what New Zealand would have been like around 2000 years ago when Te Matua Ngahere (meaning 'father of the forest') in Northland's Waipoua Forest was not much more than a seedling? Over its lifetime this magnificent kauri tree has been witness to incredible changes, not least of which have been the assorted trials and tribulations of the human population as they have come and gone — and come again to this region, and of course the destruction of the many hundreds of other kauri that once flourished up here.

There is something very special about this tree; whether you prefer to admire its unique qualities in situ as it were or to discover how the early New Zealanders chopped them down and put them to use in a variety of ways, you won't be short of opportunities to do both in the Far North.

Waipoua, Puketi and Omahuta are three remaining kauri forests, each featuring different sized trees, ranging from rickers (young trees carrying short branches up their trunks) through to huge specimens. Take a stroll through any of these forests, which are all readily accessible from paths or walking tracks, but make sure you include Waipoua Forest, home to two of New Zealand's oldest and largest living kauri: Tane Mahuta ('lord of the forest'), the tallest at 51 m, and Te Matua Ngahere, the older of the two, measuring an impressive 16.4 m around its girth.

If you want to see larger trees, you'll have to take yourself to the Kauri Museum at Matakohe, one of New Zealand's most amazing theme museums, which attracts around 85,000 visitors every year. Along with a magnificent collection of antique kauri furniture, fabulous displays include many old photographs showing just how common really gigantic specimens of *Agathis australis* once were in this part of the world. The museum also boasts the world's largest collection of kauri gum. Finish up by absorbing the following sobering statistics about this majestic species: kauri forests once covered a million hectares of the north; now only 7455 ha of mature forest remain. Three-quarters of the destruction occurred between 1800 and 1900.

Take in the tallest tree in New Zealand, Tane Mahuta, and the other kauri at Waipoua.

Wordsmiths of the capital

Wellington has so much to offer that it's best to plan a number of visits so you can concentrate on one theme at a time. Finding out about some of New Zealand's literati, from early in the twentieth century through to the present day, is a great way to spend a weekend: not only will you be able to feel virtuous after all the exercise involved, but you'll also have developed a taste for some good reading in the months and years to come.

You'll find the Wellington Writers Walk right on the waterfront, only a short distance from the hustle and bustle of the city's shopping precinct. The walk celebrates and commemorates the place of Wellington in these writers' lives, and their place in the life of this vibrant city. The purpose of the walk is to enjoy a series of quotations from these writers in the form of large concrete typographic 'text sculptures' designed by award-winning Wellington typographer and graphic designer Catherine Griffiths. But one of the reasons why this is such an enjoyable activity is that the sculptures are not always where you might expect to find them. The walk currently commemorates 19 authors, both past and present, including poets, novelists, playwrights and writers of prose. A brochure including a map of the sculpture sites is available free from libraries, bookshops and information centres.

While still in full-on literary mode, head towards the old inner-city suburb of Thorndon, where you can visit the childhood home of one of the world's best-known short-story writers. Many of Katherine Mansfield's early memories in this house, where three generations of her family lived from 1888 to 1893, feature in her short stories. The meticulously restored house at 25 (previously 11) Tinakori Road is administered by the Katherine Mansfield Birthplace Society Inc, a non-profit charitable organisation.

There's also a heritage garden that has been faithfully recreated by a team of volunteers following the evidence provided by eye-witness accounts, original photographs, archaeological investigation, and Mansfield's stories and letters.

Restoration of Katherine Mansfield's early home in Tinakori Road has been a labour of love.

Words become visual art on the
Wellington Writers Walk.

The holy trail

One of the most popular ways of seeing the very best that Central Otago has to offer is through the Otago Central Rail Trail experience or, as it's sometimes referred to, simply the Rail Trail. Whether you choose to do this family-friendly outdoor adventure by bike or on foot (some even do it on horseback), it's guaranteed to be a few days of not too strenuous exercise, lots of fantastic scenery and, depending on your budget, a range of accommodation options from backpackers' hostels to refurbished period buildings to luxury hotels.

For the most part the trail is an undulating gravelled surface with no difficult hill climbs, making it suitable for all age groups and levels of fitness. And for those in need of the occasional distraction,

there are several vineyards en route, all of which offer various forms of refreshment and, in at least one case, fairly up-market accommodation.

There's absolutely no obligation to stick to the trail, and many people choose to head off to any one of the delightful

'OK, chaps, last one to the pub buys the first round!'

One of the accommodation and refreshment stops on the trail, the Wedderburn Tavern has been fully restored.

The Rail Trail starts and/or finishes at Middlemarch, famous for its gourmet game pies.

settlements dotted about such as Poolburn, Ophir, Becks, St Bathans, Naseby, Macraes Town and Kyeburn. If a night or two in any of these places appeals and you've booked ahead, ask your host if they offer a pick-up and drop-off service, which will make the detour pleasantly hassle-free.

Then there are the pubs, cafés and restaurants along the way. There's something for every appetite, including truly scrumptious hand-made pies in Middlemarch for those who've worked up a suitably manly appetite.

The trail is 150 km in total but of course there's no obligation to do the whole thing — it's entirely up to you, including which

end you start at: Clyde or Middlemarch, both settlements that are worth spending a day or so investigating for their own charms. Most people do the trail between mid-October and April — the warmer months.

One of the main attractions of the trail is that motorised vehicles are not permitted on it so there's no fear of being forced off the track or any other unpleasant consequence of having to share the road with four-wheeled competition.

Abel Tasman National Park

ECO/
WILDERNESS

A visit to the DOC

We are so lucky here in New Zealand to have such a wealth of fabulous spots where we can get away from it all. And to have an organisation such as the Department of Conservation (DOC) running a number of campsites and other forms of accommodation up and down the country. Obviously they are very much in demand during the summer months, but with a bit of judicial planning you and your family or friends can enjoy a wonderful weekend at almost any time of the year for a fairly modest cost.

If you want to get right away and you're prepared to put in some hard physical work to get there, consider one of the 950 back-country huts that DOC has on its books. Generally they are pretty basic and you'll have to take absolutely everything you might need for the weekend because there's no chance of popping down to a shop to pick up whatever you may have forgotten.

There are also more than 250 vehicle-accessible camping areas on conservation land, many of which are on or near the coast. They are divided into three categories: serviced (flush toilets, tap water, kitchen/cooking bench, hot showers, rubbish collection, and sometimes laundry facilities, barbecues, fireplaces, cookers and picnic tables); standard (composting or pit variety toilets, water supply (via tap, stream or lake), and sometimes cold showers,

cooking shelters and rubbish bins); and basic (you'll need to be fully self-sufficient to stay at one of these).

DOC also manages a number of lodges, cabins and cottages in scenic settings nationwide. Some are more comfortable than others but they all have beds, bunks or sleeping platforms with mattresses (often enough room to accommodate a small crowd), plus table and chairs, tap water, toilets, toilet paper and a broom and brush for tidying up. Some come with a full kitchen, in which case you can cook up a storm in relative comfort, provided you've done the shopping beforehand. However, you'll need to bring your own bed linen or sleeping bags, tea towels, food and personal items in all cases.

Whichever of these options appeals, don't forget to book — you'll find all the details on DOC's website (see page 236).

Back-country hut or campsite, fabulous scenery is all just part of DOC's service. This is the Upper Travers Hut, Nelson Lakes.

Peace and tranquility at the Awaroa Hut,
Abel Tasman National Park.

Small is beautiful

Walking the Abel Tasman can be fun for all the family.

It might be New Zealand's smallest national park, but the Abel Tasman certainly makes up for it with the fabulous range of outdoor activities that you can enjoy here. It's one of those 'every bit as good as if not better' experiences promised by the glossy brochures; the colour of those golden beaches and the amazing water scenes really are that gorgeous! And in case you need further persuasion, you're likely to get more sun here than just about anywhere else in the country.

Most people visit the park to tramp all or part of the 51 km Coast Track (one of New Zealand's Great Walks), but there's also the Inland Track that leads over the highest part of the park through forest and which can be walked in three to five days. However, for those short on time, there are a few day-walks, most of which will get you near one of those glorious coves with their crystal-clear waters.

Opportunities for some great outdoor fun are plentiful in this park, which you can reach via four main gateways: Marahau and Kaiteriteri are at the southern end, accessed by road from Motueka, and the two northern entrances are at Totaranui and Wainui, reached by road from Takaka in Golden Bay. Getting to these points is no problem, thanks to regular bus services, and if you want to be picked up somewhere within the park, this can be arranged in advance with one of the commercial boat operators.

Paddling around the park's coastline is another popular option.

Apart from the sheer pleasure of walking in such a fantastic setting, you can go swimming and snorkelling; the coastline's rounded bays, estuaries, rocky headlands and small islands also make it a great place for kayaking. And if dark places are more your thing, why not explore some of the park's caves, whose inhabitants include wetas and glow-worms?

Bird watchers will find plenty to look at because the combination of habitats — marine, coastal and forest — encourages a wide diversity of birds (but watch out for those cheeky wekas!).

If you're there during the balmy summer months, you'll probably enjoy sleeping under the stars for at least one night, or maybe you'd prefer the comforts of a lodge — it's your choice.

Crossing Tongariro

So you've decided to leave an absolutely minimal carbon footprint on your next weekend away. Sounds like the 17 km Tongariro Alpine Crossing in the central North Island's Tongariro National Park could be right up your alley.

You can choose to do a guided walk or, if you want to do it on a DIY basis, you'll need to organise transport to the beginning of the track — and a pick-up at the end. It's not a walk that should be attempted unless you are fairly fit. But if you're up for it, it's a unique experience rated by many as being among the top 10 day-treks in the world.

It'll take somewhere between seven and nine hours to walk from the Mangatepopo Valley towards the Ketetahi Road end and you can expect to see some mind-boggling

The Tongariro Alpine Crossing starts between Mounts Ngauruhoe (right) and Tongariro.

natural beauty along the way such as the Emerald Lakes (so named because of their stunning colour, which is caused by minerals leached from the surrounding rock) and the Blue Lake further up the track. On a clear day the views are truly amazing and if conditions are right it is possible to see Taranaki Mount Egmont way over on the western horizon.

The weather plays a dramatic part up here, and conditions are likely to be quite different from those down below — so it pays to equip yourself with sturdy boots, warm clothing and a waterproof jacket, whatever the time of year. Obviously there's no chance of buying supplies en route, so make sure you've got plenty of water and food to keep you going.

If there's any serious doubt about the weather, you're better off finding something else to do in the area rather than risk not seeing anything or, worse yet, suffering from exposure (not an enviable state)! There are plenty of other things to do in this amazingly scenic and volcanically active region — hot pool, anyone?

As with many other 'weekend away' options, there is a range of accommodation to suit every budget — from campground huts to luxury lodges or the Grand Chateau.

Walkers are rewarded for their efforts by stunning views of the Blue Lake.

On track in Milford

How many people do you know who still have the Milford Track on their 'to do' list? Get a head start on them and make a booking to walk this iconic track now! However, if bookings are too heavy, you might want to consider one of the other fantastic tracks in the region. This part of New Zealand gets international travel writers drooling on a regular basis — there aren't that many places left in the developed world where there's just so much natural beauty on offer.

You can walk the Milford Track independently (there are three DOC huts on the track) or as part of a guided group, which will see you tucked up at night in slightly more salubrious conditions. Both options involve three nights away, not including the time it takes to get down there and back to your own neck of the woods, so don't forget to tell the boss you won't be there on Monday . . . or Tuesday, for that matter. Highlights include nine suspension bridges, a loo with the best view in Fiordland, waterfalls — and did we mention the views all along the track?

In the event that the Milford Track is booked out, consider either the Routeburn or Kepler tracks. Both are in the Te Anau area, a truly gorgeous part of the country, and the good news is that during the high season neither is as busy as the big M (but you still need to book).

Although shorter in length than the

The Sutherland Falls viewed from Quintin Huts on the Milford Track.

Trampers enjoy the rainforest scenery on the Kepler Track.

Milford, the Routeburn requires quite a high level of fitness and will take around three and a half days to complete the 32 km track through Mount Aspiring and Fiordland national parks. Highlights include impressive beech forest, ferns, mosses, lichens — and you may be lucky enough to see the endangered mohua (yellowhead/bush canary). Sparrow sized, it has a bright yellow head, neck and breast, with the rest of the body being brownish yellow.

The Kepler, a 60 km circular track traversing the spectacular scenery of Fiordland National Park, is longer but easier (allow three to four days). Fantastic forest, waterfalls and a beautiful lakeshore beach — plus opportunities for trout fishing — make this walk a very attractive option.

All three tracks are administered by DOC (see website details on page 236).

Snow business

Once our glorious summer is over, there is still lots to do in the great outdoors and each year a sizeable chunk of the population just can't wait for it to get good and cold. The reason for this is their passion for skiing — if you haven't given it a go, what are you waiting for?

Unless you live in the Far North, there's nowhere in New Zealand that's too far from a skifield so from June to November you can have a great time at any of the country's 17 commercially operated ski and snowboard areas. These days, considering the number of overseas visitors they attract, they come with world-class snow-making, snow-

grooming, and base and dining facilities.

But don't overlook the largely ski-club operated skifields in your search for a weekend on the snow. In most cases casual visitors are welcome, and although the facilities can be simple, such as a rope tow or T-bar lift, they often have good day lodges and offer a nicely social atmosphere.

There's also some magnificent back-country skiing to be had, but this is probably best avoided if you're a novice.

If you're not too far from a commercial skifield and you're going to get into the sport on a regular basis, it's worth splashing out on a season pass. But if it's

Going to the snow is fun
for kids of all ages.

Getting some air at Whakapapa on Mt Ruapehu (left) and Ohau, in the South Island.

likely to be a one-off weekend, then beg, borrow or steal everything you're likely to need and go for it!

North Island top spots include Whakapapa, Turoa and Tukino (although don't overlook Manganui, in the Egmont National Park on the slopes of Taranaki Mount Egmont — it's run on a volunteer basis and if you don't mind pitching in to help with maintenance before the season starts, you'll be very welcome there).

In the South Island, you're spoilt for choice: Hanmer Springs, Porters, Mount Hutt, Treble Cone, Cardrona and Coronet Peak to name a few. The scenery in most of these places is to die for and there is plenty of après-ski activity to keep you entertained.

If all else fails and you just can't get yourself anywhere near a real mountain, there's always Snowplanet in Auckland where you can fool around in some fairly authentic snow all year round.

Otago's wild peninsula

If you've seen enough common or garden variety seabirds to last you a while and you feel the need to see some wingspan, then pack your binoculars along with a warm jacket and some sturdy shoes and head down to the Otago Peninsula. Stretching along the southern edge of the Otago harbour, this famous eco-tourism attraction — which includes the only mainland breeding colony for any albatross species found in the southern hemisphere — has much to offer anyone with an interest in New Zealand wildlife. Royal albatross are among the star attractions here — and rightly so because with their 3 m wingspan, they are an absolutely amazing sight to behold as they soar above you.

For those who feel that their knowledge of New Zealand flora and fauna is somewhat lacking and could do with some expert input, a guided tour of the peninsula is a good option. Various operators offer tours that enable you to experience close encounters with some of the world's rarest wildlife, including some 15 to 20 species of marine and wading birds, royal albatross (the protected nature reserve has grown into an established colony with a current population of around 140 birds), Hooker's sea lions, blue penguins, New Zealand fur seals and those sweet little yellow-eyed penguins — the extremely rare hoiho — that most of us only know from television.

You don't have to restrict yourself to exploring the peninsula via terra firma — at least one tour operator runs cruises around the headlands of Taiaroa. And if you want to do it yourself, then simply hire a sea kayak and off you go.

A word of warning, however: whether you go exploring on your own or in a group, make sure you don't get too close to the wildlife. They are entitled to feel secure and you certainly don't want an angry sea lion chasing you — it's amazing how fast they can move when motivated.

While you've got the smell of the sea in your nostrils, why not pop into the

A baby albatross tries out its wings at Taiaroa Head.

The peninsula is wild and windswept, but full of hidden treasures.

New Zealand Marine Studies Centre on the harbourside of the peninsula, where the aquarium showcases marine life from southern New Zealand waters? There's an impressive amount to see here, including touch tanks where, as the aquarium's promotional material says, 'you can get your hands wet and your mind salty!' Fish feeding sessions are another interesting option, and one that is certain to appeal to children.

Seals are frequent visitors to the Otago Peninsula.

Waikaremoana wilderness

Given how much time most of us spend strapped into our cars it's little wonder that we yearn to stretch our legs in the great outdoors as often as possible. The Lake Waikaremoana Track in the North Island's Te Urewera National Park is guaranteed to get rid of most of the kinks, but could well be responsible for causing some different ones!

It's a glorious walk that follows the western edge of Lake Waikaremoana, deep in the heart of the park, and can take anywhere from a couple of days through to five days to complete (the track is 46 km long). Accommodation is provided through a number of DOC-managed campsites and huts; whichever option you choose, you *must* book beforehand.

A good-sized pack to carry everything you'll need (water, food, clothes, sleeping bag, etc. — and a portable cooking stove if you're camping) is compulsory, unless you've chosen a guided walk. These don't come cheap but all meals are provided, your heavy stuff gets carted by someone else and you'll only have to carry a daypack. What bliss!

You really should make the effort to squeeze in some fishing gear too, because there will be plenty of opportunities to try your luck in the lake (think succulent trout!). But if you'd rather watch nature than eat it, bring a pair of binoculars to make the most of the varied birdlife. The forest teems with fantails, tomtits and kereru, as well as bellbirds and tui. While you might not get to actually see a kiwi, chances are good you'll hear their night-time calls from your hut or tent as they forage in the forest.

Walking through the forest of giant rata, rimu and miro is a magical experience — at times it feels as if yours are the first human footprints to mark the ground. As you climb, the views become more and more stunning. Be sure to take some well-deserved rests along the way, especially in high summer when the cool waters of the lake will be very attractive indeed.

When you've reached the end of the track you can choose to take a water taxi back to the starting point or make other pick-up arrangements.

Choose between easing your aching feet or casting a line into the cool waters of Lake Waikaremoana.

The Panekiri Bluff rises out of the dense bush of the
Urewera National Park.

Island sanctuaries

There are times when it's great to get away from it all to a place where nature reigns supreme, albeit with a little help from some dedicated conservators. Two stunning examples of such places are Tiritiri Matangi Island, north of Auckland, and Kapiti Island, north of Wellington. In both cases a boat trip is necessary and during summer months it's essential to book.

Tiritiri Matangi, whose name means 'a place tossed by the wind', is a shining example of what can be done when a bunch of volunteers get the bit between their teeth. Between 1984 and 1994 volunteers planted close to 300,000 trees on the island, which had been seriously denuded due to many years of farming.

These days the Department of Conservation administers Tiritiri, and in the process has eradicated all mammalian predators and successfully introduced a number of species of threatened and endangered birds. These include little spotted kiwi, brown teal, takahe, red-crowned parakeet, whitehead, North Island robin, hihi (stitchbird), North Island kokako, North Island saddleback, fernbird and North Island tomtit.

Take some walking shoes and a picnic lunch and enjoy the sound of the birdlife all around you — it's a very special experience.

When making plans to visit Kapiti Island, much further down the North Island, you must organise yourself a visitor access permit, available from DOC, because only so many visitors are allowed on the island at any one time.

Like Tiritiri, Kapiti is one of a few relatively accessible island nature reserves — in fact, it is the only large island sanctuary for birds between the Hauraki Gulf in the north and New Zealand's southern outlying islands. As on Tiritiri you can see the results achieved by a bunch of dedicated people in their planting and predator eradication efforts.

Among the wide variety of forest birdlife you're likely to spot are tui, bellbird, weka, kaka, kereru and the North Island robin. Saddleback, hihi and takahe are also present and on the lagoon you'll see scaup, grey teal, and black swans. Along the shoreline at Rangatira you'll be able to spot various species of shag and gull, white-fronted terns, variable oystercatchers and reef herons.

It's a veritable bird watchers' paradise (but keep an eye out for the cheeky weka and kaka any time you put down your bag; they'll be into it so quickly you won't know what's hit you!).

You can visit Kapiti only if you have an official visitor access permit.

This good-looking takahe on Tiritiri Matangi Island makes the most of a tailwind.

Lake Dunstan, Central Otago

FAMILY FUN

Back to basics with the kids

Weekends and school holidays can be an expensive business when you've got kids clamouring to be entertained — and that's not counting petrol and other less obvious costs. So the last thing you want to be doing is shelling out your hard-earned dollars on expensive activities when, with a bit of judicious research, you and your family can have a great time at very little cost.

New Zealand has way more than its share of green spaces: from the local parks that are generally not far from most urban households to a series of fabulously scenic reserves all over the country. Take Auckland: it has 26 regional parks on its doorstep, each offering a great outdoor experience that can be as simple as a picnic, maybe a swim and a bit of a walk, or even full-on camping. The lower end of the North Island is not without some wonderful outdoor spaces, either — Wellington, for example, is lucky enough to have an inviting green belt that's just full of spots to explore. The South Island has, if anything, even more fantastic outdoor options, many of which are handy to the towns and cities (think

Building sandcastles on the beach is one of New Zealand's simple pleasures.

There's a green space near you, such as Pukekura Park in New Plymouth, and it doesn't cost the earth.

Hagley Park in Christchurch).

During more inclement weather indoor activities are often preferable — fortunately just about every good-sized centre will have a museum of some kind. You could even make a point of visiting all those within, say, a two-hour drive from your home. The variety will astound you.

City-slicker families probably enjoy the idea of getting up close and personal with some farm animals, but they need to make sure they have the blessing of the farmer before letting the kids loose in a paddock. Alternatively, many smaller centres have a petting zoo; they may not be free but the charge is generally quite reasonable.

Feeding everyone during the day doesn't have to cost an arm and a leg, either. Make it a family affair from start to finish and get the kids to help you make up a yummy picnic the day or night before (cold sausage or bacon and egg pie, anyone?).

Family fun can be educational, too, at museums such as Taranaki's Puke Ariki.

Cast, catch, then cook

The excitement of catching a *Salmo trutta* or *Oncorhynchus mykiss* (that's brown and rainbow trout respectively to the likes of you and me) is hard to beat, but imagine how much easier it could be if you bone up on some basic trout information to enhance your chances of success before you even get out your rod.

That's where the Tongariro National Trout Centre comes in. Officially opened in 2003 and situated a little south of Turangi, the centre is dedicated to supporting and encouraging angling in the Tongariro–Taupo area — by providing information about how and where wild trout live and the different ways to fish for them. Through the centre's activities, you'll quickly become aware of the importance of sustainability, so future generations can also enjoy fishing in the region (the centre also regularly works with many schools on this topic). Attractively landscaped with natural stone, the centre comprises an auditorium and display area, an underwater viewing chamber and a hatchery. Got the kids with you? No problem — they are going to love feeding the fish in the children's fishing pond, and if you time your visit right, they can learn fly-rod skills from the centre's volunteers (do find out in advance when this activity is on offer).

While you're there, take a stroll along the Tongariro River. The River Walk Visitor Centre is full of interesting displays and information about the Taupo trout fishery. When the need to sit down and partake of some refreshment comes over you, you can take advantage of the coin-operated barbecue and picnic facilities.

After your session here, the hardest thing will be to decide just where in nearby Lake Taupo you want to cast your rod and catch your very own succulent brown trout (once you've got your licence, that is). There are also a number of trout-packed rivers in the central North Island including the Tauranga-Taupo, Waipunga, Mohaka and Whakapapa rivers.

If you're planning on sharing your trout, dazzle your fellow diners with some fishy facts such as that rainbow trout eat more and grow faster than brown trout; that in lakes, they tend to live in deeper water and that they are more easily caught than the wary brown trout.

Happy fishing!

Ice-cold water to your thighs? All in a day's work for the keen angler.

The children's fishing pool gets them started young.

Escape to the bach

A warm day, a good book — what more could you possibly want?

For those of us who have yet to win Lotto, our very own holiday home remains a dream. But a weekend holiday home experience in one of New Zealand's many idyllic holiday spots — whether for just the two of you or a large family group — can now be yours at the click of a mouse.

In recent years a whole string of dedicated websites listing holiday homes for rent have sprung up — most have photographs so you know exactly what you're getting and you can search by location, by size, by availability, or by cost.

Beachfront properties are, naturally, very popular, however they don't come cheap; but if you're prepared for a bit of a walk to get to the water, you could save yourself quite a lot of money. Facilities and levels of comfort vary, too — from one-bedroom accommodation with a pull-out sofa bed in the main living area and maybe some bunk beds in the garage to seriously stylish architecturally designed luxury pads complete with gold taps and white leather furniture. Then there are all those in between, which are generally most in demand.

Some of the most popular locations in the upper North Island include Coromandel, Waiheke Island and, of course, all those gloriously golden beaches on the east coast north of Auckland as far as Doubtless Bay. Then there's Taupo and various other hot spots such as Hawke's Bay and the

Baches or cribs, such as this one at Lake Alexandrina in the Mackenzie Country, come in all shapes and sizes.

The Moonlight Bach at Scandrett Regional Park, north of Auckland, encapsulates the Kiwi bach experience.

Wairarapa. The South Island offers plenty of options, too with Nelson/Golden Bay and Marlborough being among the favoured locations.

When you book a bach through an established organisation, it's generally easy to find out exactly what you're getting for your money, especially in terms of what you may or may not need to bring. BYO bed linen is normal practice as are BYO food and drink. Some places may be amenable to you using their basics such as salt, pepper, detergent, etc — but if you start making inroads into any of the owner's supplies it's only fair to replace them.

Common to pretty well all rented holiday accommodation is the expectation that you leave the property as you found it, i.e. clean and tidy — or you'll face extra costs.

Country comes to town

Thinking about a weekend away in early winter? Then shake out your gumboots and your most authentic-looking rural rainwear and head to the Waikato for Fieldays (or to give it its proper moniker: the New Zealand National Agricultural Fieldays) to see the latest in farming innovations and new technology in a rural context. Hard to imagine that this four-day event, which now attracts well in excess of 100,000 people a year, had such modest beginnings back in 1969 at Te Rapa Racecourse with a budget of just $10,500.

Nowadays of course it's held at Mystery Creek, near Hamilton Airport, and is the biggest agricultural showcase in the southern hemisphere, featuring large machinery, livestock feeds, milking equipment and ostrich products among many other things.

Along with all the usual displays, live entertainment and competitions that you'd expect to find at such an event there are some that are rather more unusual. For example, if you're in the market for a handy bloke or woman in your life, then be sure to introduce yourself to those on the shortlist of the Fieldays Rural Bachelor of the Year award, who, in order to be eligible to enter, must be 18 or older, work in the rural sector and 'exude understated Kiwi charm'. Recently the competition was expanded to include female challengers.

Other quirky competitions worth a look include the Fieldays No. 8 Wire National Art Award, hosted by the ArtsPost gallery. Entrants may twist, bend or weld lengths of this iconic wire (or a 4 mm soft galvanised wire equivalent) to achieve a sculptural work of art. There's also the Ag Art Wear and Possum Fur Fashion Design awards, which encourage rural designers to look beyond the traditional farming favourites (i.e. gumboots and Swanndris). The main criterion for these competitions is that the wearable art must be made from items found on the farm. Previous entries have featured bodices made of clay targets and dog biscuits, outfits made of shotgun shells, hats fashioned from barbed wire and pretty necklaces of artificial insemination straws.

After Fieldays you're guaranteed to see farmers — and farming — in an entirely different light.

Tractor racing is a popular event at the annual Fieldays.

Farmers and families swarm to Mystery Creek each year for a nosey.

Follow the underground stars

Next time it's dark and you're hungry, try shining a torch around and see if a snack presents itself. This method certainly works for glow-worms (which aren't actually worms at all; they're the larvae of the carnivorous fungus gnat), though there's no guaranteed success for the rest of us. Maybe we should just stick to admiring the way they congregate on dark and generally damp surfaces, waiting patiently for their supper of midges, mayflies and caddis flies, and in the process creating a spectacle that can be compared to a clear star-filled night sky.

Although they can be found in many places throughout New Zealand, they can be seen to fantastic effect in the North Island's Waitomo Caves and the South Island's Te Anau Glow-worm Caves. Both locations involve exploring by path as well as by boat and in high season it makes sense to book ahead to avoid disappointment.

A visit to the Te Anau Glow-worm Caves is enhanced by a cruise across the lake itself to where the caves are located on the somewhat isolated western side. Although these caves, not surprisingly, featured strongly in local Maori legend it wasn't until 1948 that explorer Lawson Burrows 'discovered' them. Before you head underground, there'll be plenty of

The dramatic entrance to the Ruakuri Cave at Waitomo.

Visitors to Te Anau's Glow-worm Caves prepare to be dazzled.

101 MUST-DO WEEKENDS

The Waitomo Caves give visitors the chance to get up close to glow-worm threads.

opportunity to find out more about these luminous little larvae via the informative displays at Cavern House.

Although the whole expedition only takes two and a quarter hours — including the trip across the lake — you're in one of the most beautiful places in New Zealand, so there's no shortage of other things to see and do over the weekend.

When you plan your visit to the Waitomo Caves you can choose between a couple of tour options. One will take you down into the gigantic cavern otherwise known as the Cathedral, where the quality of the acoustics has attracted the likes of Dame Kiri Te Kanawa to sing, and the deep limestone shaft known as the Tomo. Then, in a boat you'll drift silently through the Glow-worm Grotto where whole galaxies of glow-worms will light up the way.

An alternative tour will guide you off the beaten track and away from the busier caves to a couple of large caves on private conservation reserves; a raft ride to appreciate the magical display is part of this experience.

Petrolhead heaven

Calling all petrolheads! At last there's a venue where you can indulge your passion for a no-holds-barred barrage of noise and fumes. Since 2008, Hamilton — in the heart of New Zealand's largest dairy-producing region — has claimed the 400 V8 Supercar Championships as its own. This medium-sized provincial city now goes all out to make it a truly fun outing for all the family.

Taking place over three days, the event comprises a colourful mix of motor racing and non-stop entertainment including a beauty contest (the Samsung Miss Hamilton 400 competition) and assorted rugby games — all set amid a carnival atmosphere that's as appealing to families as it is to motor-racing enthusiasts. This is such a popular event you'll need to secure accommodation well in advance.

It starts with a practice day (perfect for novices to get their heads around the concept of it all); nearly 38,000 people turned up for the preliminaries at the most recent event. The turnout for the high-speed action main events is usually similarly impressive. Around 30 teams are involved, with participants coming from all over. So what can you expect to see? For the uninitiated, the circuit length is 3.4 km and runs clockwise. The average speed reached is 141 km/h and the maximum speed to date is 248 km/h. And the cars? Big grunty Fords and Holdens rule the event.

There are seven major grandstands from which to view the action, but if you feel the need to have some quiet time between events, head for the Hamilton Gardens where a peaceful wander through the attractively themed displays will soon have you up to speed and ready for more high-octane action.

Conservationists take note: all V8 Supercars now run on 85 per cent CSR Ethanol, a renewable fuel made from the by-product of the sugar refining process.

Ford fans show their colours at the Hamilton 400.

Fans come from all over to witness the speed, thrills and spills.

Home on the road

Perhaps all you'll hear when you go to bed is the rustle of night creatures or maybe just the sound of the sea; it all depends how far away you want to get. In any event a weekend in a campervan or motorhome can see you ending up in any number of places — that's the beauty of these self-contained mini-homes on wheels.

They come in all shapes and sizes and so can accommodate anything from an intimate twosome to a combination of adults and children — but if it's the latter, you want to choose your time of year carefully. If the heavens open for much of the weekend it won't be any fun for you or the kids to be cooped up together in a small space!

So assuming all conditions are favourable, what are your options in terms of a destination? Well, just about any place that appeals to you and which is motor-home-friendly is the short answer. In the greater Auckland area, just visiting the regional parks — many situated in highly scenic locations — could conceivably take up most weekends over a year. Further south there are rivers and lakes to explore plus beaches of all shapes, colours and sizes. And don't overlook DOC's magnificent network of national parks and reserves; their prime purpose is to be explored and enjoyed by New Zealanders, so check out one near you.

If doing anything highly physical is not on the agenda, point your vehicle in the direction of a wine region such as Matakana, Hawke's Bay or Martinborough in the North Island and spend a couple of days tasting your way around (after you've appointed a responsible driver, of course!). In the South Island gorgeous grapes and their by-products can be found in Marlborough, Nelson, Waipara/Canterbury and Central Otago.

Town, country or beachside, you get to choose where you'll sleep tonight.

Kids going crazy

Sometimes kids need something to get their adrenalin levels fizzing — and collecting shells or going to a museum just isn't going to cut the mustard.

In Auckland there's Rainbow's End, which will have the kids hopping with excitement as they wait their turn on assorted rides including the dreaded Fear Fall, Pirate Ship, Cam Am Cars and Log Flume rides, or the more sedate Bumper Boats, Dodgems and Roller Coaster. An hour or so north on the motorway is Snowplanet, where your offspring can snowboard to their hearts' content. Roughly in between those two you'll find Kelly Tarlton's Underwater World.

Further down country the Bay of Plenty has enough to keep the kids occupied for much more than just a weekend. Start off with a day at Tauranga's Waimarino Adventure Park, where pedalos (boat rides), rock climbing, kayaking, beach volleyball and the park's low ropes course will keep them happy for hours.

The next day, move on to Rotorua's Agrodome and introduce the kids to goats, cattle, deer, alpacas and ostriches. If that's too tame, the same venue offers thrill-seeking activities such as bungy jumping, the legendary Zorb, the wicked Swoop, Freefall Xtreme body flying, Agrojet, Shweeb rides, Helipro and much more.

Prepare for things to get messy in Wellington, where the Paintball Adventure Challenge uses latest technology weapons, environmentally safe, non-staining vegetable dyes and challenging combat courses and combat zones that older children in particular will enjoy.

Don't forget the International Antarctic Centre in Christchurch, where kids can experience snow and ice as well as learn amazing facts about the frozen continent through interactive displays. If they still need cooling off, head to Christchurch's Alpine Ice, where the whole family can skate to the latest sounds plus enjoy a funky light display.

Kids will love the big chill at the International Antarctic Centre in Christchurch.

Finish up in Christchurch with a visit to Adrenalin Forest —an adventure and playing field in the heart of the forest with several levels of difficulty and which offers fun for the whole family.

For something different, Stuart Landsborough's Puzzling World in Wanaka claims to have the world's first 'modern-styled' great maze, along with incredible illusion rooms, a puzzle centre/café and assorted eccentric architecture and oddities. Not far away is the Cardrona Adventure Park, which offers an obstacle course driven by a monster truck that's the world's biggest school bus, family quad-bike rides, go-karts, extreme eight-wheel argo rides, and other stunt rides.

And although there's less energy expended, you can't go to Dunedin without visiting Cadbury World — the name says it all!

A downhill ride in a Zorb at Rotorua will wake the kids up.

Full of hot air

If you consider the number of regular crowd-pulling events in Hamilton, then maybe the city's claim of 'Hamilton is where it happens' is not too far from the truth. Though this provincial city has been involved with a balloon festival of one kind or another every year since 1988, in 1999 the Balloons over Waikato Charitable Trust was set up to make it official and provide new direction and continuity.

Now billed as the nation's premier hot-air balloon festival, the five-day event attracts balloonists from all over New Zealand and around the world to demonstrate their skills in a range of competitive activities. Most of the activity centres on Innes Common on Lake Domain Drive, next to Hamilton Lake, where the balloons are launched early in the morning. Watching them inflate is fascinating in itself, with the larger balloons taking up to 40 minutes to fill. Once up in the air, their direction is dictated by the wind and they usually stay up for between one and two hours at a time. However, if you can't get to the common to watch them take off, chances are you'll see them floating sedately across the sky wherever you happen to be in Hamilton (although if you spot them while driving, the organisers recommend pulling over to watch them — to avoid being dangerously distracted).

Day one of the festival begins with a mass ascension in which up to 35 balloons

How is the air up there? Visitors take to the skies at Hamilton's balloon festival.

of all shapes and sizes, some quite spectacular, lift off from the common. Over the next four days, the balloons participate in various fun events, one of the highlights of which is the Nightglow show. Starting late afternoon in the grounds of the University of Waikato, this family-friendly programme features a host of live acts that perform over several hours as a build-up to a stunning light and sound show starring the balloons themselves.

Should the urge to enjoy your own balloon ride prove too much to resist, commercial rides — usually lasting around an hour — are available throughout the festival.

Balloons rise at dawn into the Waikato sky.

Hitting the trail

Two wheels are nearly always better than four when it comes to family fun and if the kids are old enough to steer a bike reasonably competently, you just have to go mountain biking in Rotorua. If it suits you to transport your own bikes and equipment and map your own route trails, then go for it, but you can also hire everything you need — from the bikes themselves through to accessories such as helmets, full finger gloves, and knee, shin and elbow pads.

The tourist centre of Rotorua in the Bay of Plenty has many kilometres of purpose-built mountain biking trails (among the oldest in the country) that will satisfy riders of all abilities, from novice to expert, child or adult. Some of the most popular are in the spectacular Whakarewarewa forest known as 'The Redwoods'. Maps available from the Redwoods gift shop and visitor centre will help you figure out the trail best suited to your family's abilities. Here some 90 km of trails wind their way through lush native ferns beneath soaring forest canopies of redwood, radiata, Douglas fir, eucalyptus and larch. Along the way you'll get glimpses of Rotorua's magnificent lakes, geothermal activity and the not-too-distant Mount Tarawera.

For family groups who are anxious to keep riding on the main road to a minimum, the beginners' tracks within the network can be accessed from the main carpark on Waipa State Mill Road. Then it's just a matter of making the most of these wide, sweeping trails with their gentle climbs and descents. After a bit of practice many beginners will feel ready, as their confidence and ability increase, to move on to some of the more challenging tracks, with their mix of riding surfaces. Get the kids to check off track names as you pass them: with names like Forget Me Not, Sweet and Sour, Chop Suey and Rude Not To, you could make quite a game of it.

All the family can enjoy the trails at The Redwoods near Rotorua.

Rotorua's mountain bike trails offer great views and a variety of terrain.

In plane view

Since the first airshow way back in 1988, the skies of Central Otago have reverberated more than a few times to the sounds of some major aerial action. Now firmly established as a biennial event (the next show is be in 2010), Warbirds Over Wanaka was established by aviation enthusiast and pioneer Sir Tim Wallis, and claims to be the largest military airshow in the southern hemisphere. As with similarly large events, the show has many other complementary activities but the stars are undoubtedly the planes themselves. These which range from the biplanes of yesteryear, lovingly restored and maintained, through to the big jets of the twenty-first century.

Among the various ground displays is one showcasing military vehicles and vintage machinery —always a great hit with the kids. It's very much a live display, featuring actors in realistic uniforms using vehicles from two world wars, including big armoured tanks that are constantly on the move plus classic fire engines, steam engines, tractors and more.

Make sure you get there on the first day so you can have a good look at everything on offer in the 60-plus trade sites making up the Aviation Trade Expo and market. Depending on your budget you could make a modest investment in a plastic kitset model or go the whole hog and splash out on your own plane.

For those who know their aircraft, an impressive line-up over the years has included a Bleriot X1 and a Fokker Dr.1 from World War I, as well as more sophisticated World War II aircraft such as a Supermarine Spitfire, a Hawker Hurricane, a North American Aviation P-51D Mustang, a Curtis P-40 Kittyhawk, a Polikarpov I-16 and I-153, a Vought Corsair, a de Havilland Vampire, a Consolidated Catalina, a de Havilland Tiger Moth and a Douglas DC3/C47, among others. More recent aircraft include an MX2, a Thunder Mustang and even a gyrocopter.

Once you think you've seen it all, prepare to be amazed by a fantastic fly-by featuring the aircraft of the Royal New Zealand Air Force.

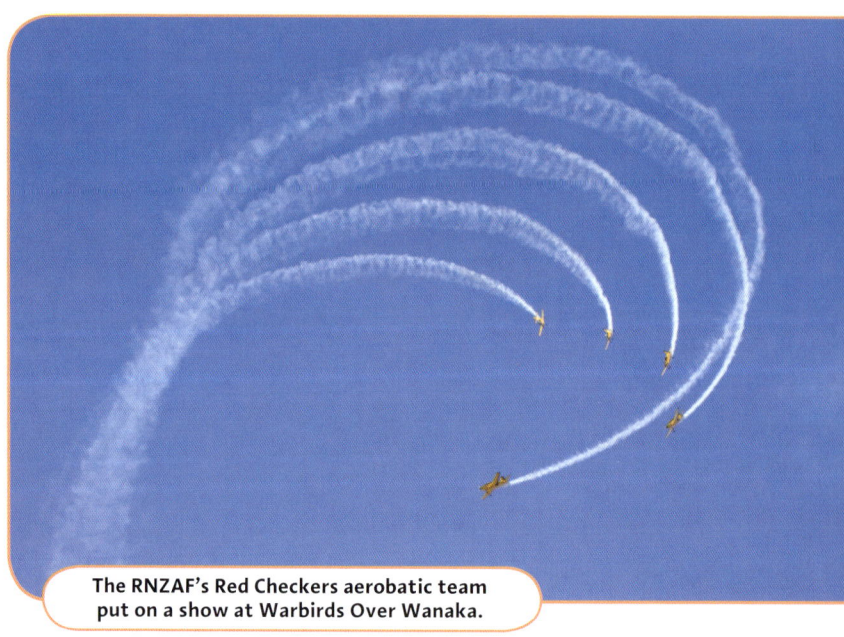

The RNZAF's Red Checkers aerobatic team put on a show at Warbirds Over Wanaka.

This World War II Hawker Hurricane is one of the stars of the show.

Fun under canvas

Whether as adults or children, nights spent under canvas are usually among our fondest memories. But why not add to your memory bank with some new camping experiences? Despite widespread development eating up some of New Zealand's camping grounds (aka holiday parks), or motorcamps as some of us remember them, there are still over 200 in the North Island and a similar number in the South, so one of them can't be too far from you!

How do you decide? Well, you could always choose one that belongs to the Holiday Parks Association of New Zealand, in which case it must be of a certain standard. Equally, those belonging to a chain such as Top 10 Holiday Parks will have a reputation to keep up. This chain operates not 10 as you might think, but 49 different grounds around the country (26 in the North Island and 23 in the South). Each one has children's play areas, barbecues and safe

Even the backdrop is beautiful at DOC's Fletcher Bay campground on the Coromandel.

Bring your thermals to camp at Glentanner, with a stunning view of Aoraki Mount Cook.

indoor and outdoor recreational areas; some have additional facilities such as tennis courts, swimming pools, spa pools and even jumping pillows (large air-filled pillows used and abused in a similar way to trampolines). They also offers lots of useful information on activities in the area you choose and their user-friendly website shows you at a glance the range of facilities available at each park. But sorry, Rover — you can't come to any of these parks.

The Kiwi Holiday Parks chain has a similar number of holiday parks throughout New Zealand. Their website is also very easy to navigate so it's a straightforward matter to find a campground within their network that will work for your family's circumstances. Certain campgrounds within this chain will allow you to bring Rover, too.

For those looking for fewer frills but who want stunning locations, DOC manages around 250 camping areas on conservation land in places as diverse as a kauri forest, islands accessible only by boat, lakesides and beachfronts, as well as national parks and other gazetted areas. Most are accessible by car. Facilities at DOC's more remote camping grounds are somewhat limited, particularly regarding rubbish collection, so you must take away absolutely everything you bring with you.

Explore our volcanoes

Did you know that among Auckland's claims to fame is that it is situated on a volcanic field? There are actually 48 volcanic cones — go, on count 'em — in Auckland and in some cases they've been there for up to 140,000 years. Locals and regular visitors to the city will be familiar with the likes of Rangitoto and One Tree Hill, but others aren't so obvious. Those that have been quarried away, like Albert Park or Mount Smart or the one that was done away with altogether in the process of developing the city's airport. Then there are those that have always just been a large hole in the ground, like Panmure and Orakei basins.

You may not have the time or inclination to traipse up, around or over each cone — or what remains of them — but some warrant exploration, especially those that happen to have some lovely grassy areas overlooking a splendid view, thus making the perfect picnic spot. Among these would have to be Mount Victoria, One Tree Hill and Maungawhau Mount Eden, which, at 196 m, is the highest —on foot it's a steep climb but well worth it for the view once you get up there.

A bit of energy — plus a boat trip — is also required to absorb the features of Rangitoto, the youngest of Auckland's volcanoes, which made its appearance in the Hauraki Gulf not much more than 600 years ago.

Orakei and Panmure basins were also once craters but were subsequently infiltrated with sea water — a very convenient development given Auckland's preoccupation with boats over the last 100 years or so. Over on the North Shore, it's been speculated that Lake Pupuke — a popular recreational spot — was formed by lava flowing back into a collapsed crater, which then filled with fresh water.

So go on, find yourself a hill somewhere in Auckland and chances are you'll have found the remnants of a volcano.

Auckland's volcanic cones offer stunning views of the city, such as this vista from Mount Eden.

Many of the cones retain their interesting archaeological features, such as these earthworks on Mangere Mountain.

Queen Charlotte Sound, Marlborough

SCENIC SPLENDOUR

Paddle for adventure

One way to escape the din of the twenty-first century for a weekend is to borrow or invest in a kayak, a lifejacket and a few other essentials, and paddle your way down one of New Zealand's most scenic rivers. You don't even have to buy the gear if you don't want to — it's all available for hire from various tourism ventures operating near the river, which is, if you haven't already guessed, the majestic Whanganui.

It's the longest navigable river in the country and on its journey to the sea it passes through the native tree- and fern-clad hills of the Whanganui National Park, making it an irresistible journey if you're halfway handy with a paddle.

You can leave your car in town or arrange to have it safely stored wherever you start or finish your trip — anything's possible if you're happy to pay for it. Depending on whether you organise your own trip or opt for a guided version, you'll sleep under canvas or in huts located at convenient points along the river (if you plan to camp you'll need a DOC hut and campsite pass, as you are passing through a national park). Common to both experiences will be the opportunity to sit under the stars at night and listen to the nocturnal sounds of morepork and kiwi — memories to cherish when you're back in the middle of civilisation with human-created noise all around you.

A trip down the river can take as long as you wish — and for the record, a kayak is an enclosed one-person craft while a canoe is open and carries two people (one paddling in the front and the other paddling at the back), plus a lot of equipment.

Paddling your own canoe is the ideal — and in some sections, the only — way to explore the natural and historic wonders of the Whanganui River.

Life's a beach

The beaches at Cathedral Cove Reserve might be small but they are perfectly formed.

If you were to ask a bunch of upper North Islanders to compile a list of their favourite beaches, chances are Hahei on the Coromandel Peninsula would feature somewhere near the top of that list. While there's been a lot of development in the area in recent years, the settlement of Hahei is still relatively small — and the beach is stunningly representative of all that is wonderful about the New Zealand coastline, especially its eastern beaches.

Golden sand on which to bake; the requisite pohutukawa positioned conveniently for shade; clean, sparkling water that's safe for swimming and boating — what more could you want apart from a large bottle of sunblock and a fabulous picnic? OK, there are spectacular views, too — of offshore islands you might want to circumnavigate via kayak. There's also some history, with an ancient Maori pa at the southern end of the beach.

For those with energy to burn and a desire to see what thousands of years of weather can do to a large chunk of sandstone, there's a brisk one and a half hour return walk (from Hahei) to Cathedral Cove. The impressively large natural rock arch located here gives the cove its name and separates two small but idyllic beaches, where you'll probably want to have a dip and then lounge around for a bit while you summon up the energy for the return walk. The waters around here are part of

Hahei is a popular bach and boating community.

Te Whanganui-a-Hei, a 9 km square marine reserve gazetted in 1993, so some snorkelling gear wouldn't go amiss.

Should the sun be unkind enough to disappear for any length of time and the temperatures drop accordingly, grab a spade and head to Hot Water Beach, just a few kilometres down the road. Here you can dig yourself a hole in the sand that will very obligingly and very speedily fill with impressively hot water from the thermal springs lurking beneath. Just be sure to time your visit to coincide with low tide.

Deciding whether to help dig or just enjoy watching others at Hot Water Beach can be a dilemma.

Sound of the south

Even though it's unlikely you'll get to see the splendours of Milford Sound without the company of a busload or three of assorted domestic and overseas tourists, it's still a sight that every Kiwi should see at least once in their lives. Europeans have been coming to gawk for many years, particularly since the Homer Tunnel was opened in 1954, thus allowing road access to this highly scenic spot.

Although quite a few Kiwis might scoff at the idea of hopping on a bus when they can drive themselves, many people choose to come here via coach — an 'all care and no responsibility' approach that means you don't have to worry about getting lost en route, running out of time to stop to drink in the scenery along the way, or finding a park among all the coaches when you arrive.

By far the best known of all of the fiords and the only one that can be accessed by road, Milford Sound is about 16 km from the head of the fiord to the open sea. The opportunity to take a cruise out to the ocean and back again is definitely one of the drawcards. Choosing a cruise to suit should be no problem, as a number of operators

Once you're out on Milford Sound itself, it's easy to forget about all those tourist buses in the car park.

offer trips from one and three-quarter hours to three hours; some include a visit to the Milford Deep Observatory — located in Harrison's Cove, where an underwater observatory provides viewing of the fiord's famous black coral and underwater life. You'll also see seals, penguins and dolphins.

According to Maori legend, the sound was carved out by Tu-te-raki-whanoa, an atua (god) who carved out the Fiordland coast. However it came to be, it's as stunning — and as wet — now as it was back when local Maori came here to collect pounamu (greenstone). All that rain (182 days of it every year) creates a series of spectacular waterfalls both at Milford Sound and along the Milford Road, a route that is gloriously scenic whatever the weather.

You'll probably get wet, but the water of the Stirling Falls is about as pure as it gets.

Tremendous train trips

It's always great to be independent, especially when you're on the move, but sometimes it's nice to just sit back and take in the view. Travelling by train is one of the very best ways to do this and the options in a region such as Canterbury really do spoil you for choice. You can even get there by train via the TranzCoastal, which connects with the Interislander ferry.

New Zealand trains have come a long way over the years and these scenic trips take place in carriages that are fêted as 'sleek, comfortable and relaxing'. Don't be in too much of a hurry to reach Christchurch: as you roll over the plains and then the narrow strip between the Pacific Ocean and the rugged, steep Kaikoura Ranges on the east coast, you may want to consider disembarking for 24 hours at Kaikoura to make the most of the unique aquatic activities available. The pick of these is, of course, whale watching, with the added bonus of seeing seals and dolphins at work and at play. The next part of the trip crosses the north Canterbury Plains, and then hey presto — you're in Christchurch.

It's your choice as to what you do before your next train trip but if you're a serious train buff, why not pay a visit to the Canterbury Railway Society, based at Ferrymead Heritage Park in Christchurch? The society restores and operates New Zealand's finest collection of steam, diesel and electric locomotives, rolling stock, signalling equipment and buildings.

The next train trip has been hailed as one of the top six rail journeys in the world. It's not that long at four and a half hours one way, but a trip in the TranzAlpine from Christchurch to Greymouth on the West Coast (and back if you choose) with its 16 tunnels and 5 viaducts is a fabulous experience, especially seen from the open-air viewing carriage. The restful vista of the Canterbury Plains, the spectacular gorges and river valleys of the Waimakariri, the majesty of the Southern Alps and the mysteriously beautiful beech forest as you approach Greymouth will remind you just why you live in our largely unspoiled country — and why so many people from the other side of the world love to visit it.

The TranzAlpine at Springfield Station, on the Canterbury Plains.

The TranzAlpine cruises thorough picture-postcard South Island scenery.

Island life

Did you know that in the maritime park that makes up the Bay of Islands there are close to 150 islands, ranging in size from mere protuberances through to sizeable chunks on which you could fit a good-sized town? Fortunately, though, the majority of them remain quite unspoilt by towns — good-sized or otherwise.

While it would be nice to explore this magnificent area in your own craft, there are so many boat trips available — including self-skippered options — you'll find yourself spoilt for choice. If you're strapped for time, there's something called a Mack Attack — powered by two 660 hp turbo-charged diesel motors that reach speeds of up to 50 knots or 100 km/h — that will get you out into the bay and back again in record time. The rest can choose

between spending anything from a day to a week on a range of craft including high-speed luxury catamarans, keelers, maxi yachts, ferries and launches — there's even an eco-cruise option.

With so many islands sprinkled throughout the area, there is no shortage of destinations and aquatic activities in which to indulge, such as swimming with dolphins, snorkelling, plain swimming of course, nature walks on some of the islands or just lazing on the beach.

Among the most popular attractions is the 'Hole in the Rock' at Motukokako Island, off Cape Brett, a narrow space through which a variety of boats regularly pass, the larger ones taking some skill to do so. Depending on which cruise operator you're booked with, you're likely to stop at Urupukapuka

Even in this popular holiday destination, you can still find secluded anchorages such as Roberton Island.

With so many islands to explore, sea kayaking can be the way to go.

Island, the largest island in the bay. This is where, back in the 1920s, American big-game fisherman and author Zane Grey established a base at Otehei Bay. These days Urupukapuka is a recreational reserve with camping grounds and a café to cater for holidaymakers and passing marine traffic.

Also popular is the iconic 'Cream Trip', based on a historic launch trip that used to collect cream from dairy farms on a number of the islands in the region and at the same time drop off mail and supplies. Although there's no more cream to be collected, the run is ongoing on a commercial sightseeing basis.

Launching luxury

The wind in your hair, the sound of the sea all around, and an ice-cold G&T in your hand hold great appeal for most of us, and one way to combine these experiences is to charter a boat for the weekend. Sailboat or launch, it's up to you, but among the very best places to experience several days on board would have to be the Hauraki Gulf and the Marlborough Sounds: both have such fantastic coastlines to explore.

In both locations there's a great choice of charter vessels. In the South Island, Picton is usually the starting point, although you can also arrange to take over your vessel in Portage and Havelock; in Auckland the boat will probably be berthed at either Westhaven, the Viaduct or Gulf Harbour.

So do you see yourself sailing or motoring? You'll need to decide early on what kind of vessel you want to charter and whether to skipper it yourself (this is known as a bareboat charter), or if you wish it can come with a skipper (as well as a valet, a cook, or perhaps a diving instructor for that matter — it all depends on the depth of your purse).

Whichever option you choose, you'll find the boat comes with everything needed to sail, anchor and operate it. Hot

Head off into the Hauraki Gulf on a voyage of discovery.

and cold running water and refrigeration are usually standard as are towels, sheets and bedding. Snorkelling gear is also usual and some yachts have dinghies with outboard motors. As for food and drink, most charter companies provide an optional provisioning service that involves delivering supplies to the yacht.

It just remains for you to decide where to sail: the Hauraki Gulf is full of attractive options, including many islands and secluded coves in which to anchor — or perhaps try your hand at fishing.

Down in the Marlborough Sounds the cruising is equally magnificent but perhaps the area is a touch more unspoiled. Cook up a barbecue on board or go ashore and enjoy a meal at one of the luxury resorts scattered along the coastline; anchor in a gorgeous bay and wake up to the birdsong — it's a tough job but someone's got to do it.

> You'll love the secluded waters of the Marlborough Sounds.

A coastal secret

For a small country New Zealand still has many largely unpopulated and therefore unspoiled places to enjoy — and the Catlins, southeast of Balclutha in the South Island, has to rate amongst the best of these. What's more, the opportunity to see so much wildlife in its natural habitat makes it an eco-tourist's dream.

The area, which takes its name from Edward Cattlin, a ship's captain who made a land claim here in 1840 (interestingly, somewhere along the way his name lost a 't'), offers an almost unparalleled variety of forests, waterfalls, coast and views over open rolling farmland. Then there's the wildlife — sea lions on the beach doing convincing impressions of large pieces of driftwood until they move (at which point you should make sure you are not too close); fur seals frolicking in and out of the water or basking in the sun; and elephant seals that have come ashore to rest or moult. At Curio Bay you can spot Hector's dolphins playing in the surf, particularly during the summer months, blissfully unaware of their endangered status. Yellow-eyed penguins are also among the regular beach-goers.

For bird watchers the Catlins is heaven on a stick. You can see shags along the coast and river edges, gulls and terns close to shore, muttonbirds, gannets and mollyhawks further out, and waders including herons, stilts, godwits and oystercatchers in the harbours and estuaries. Beady-eyed observers may even spot fernbirds and bitterns in the rushes at or just above the high-tide level.

In the forest are bellbirds, fantails, tomtits, tui and pigeons. Once you drag yourself away from the beach you'll also be able to see flowering trees like kamahi and fuchsia; ancient podocarp trees such as totara, rimu, matai and miro; plus orchids, grasses, perching plants and 28 species of fern.

There are any number of rewarding walks in the area — from a short stroll to a major trek — and there's a very good chance that on many of the routes you won't come across another living soul. (Rumour has it that during the season some of the best places for whitebaiting can be found down here, too.)

Search for fossilised treasure at Curio Bay.

Wild and wonderful Purakaunui Bay features the highest cliffs in the Catlins.

Cruise strait through

Although in this day of cheap airfares it's easy to jump on a plane when you want to hop from the North Island to the South or vice versa, why not take the time to appreciate what actually separates them by taking a return trip on the Interislander ferry service? The 92 km trip between Wellington and Picton takes about three hours and has been hailed as 'one of the most beautiful ferry rides in the world' by at least one glossy overseas magazine.

Leaving from Wellington, you'll cruise across the harbour to the waters of Cook Strait and on the way get a chance to appreciate the location of the country's capital city, nestled as it is between the hills and the water. After a short time in open waters, you'll approach Picton via Queen Charlotte Sound in the heart of the Marlborough Sounds, with its sparkling clear waters bordered by lush forests. The return journey takes the same route but in reverse.

Interislander runs three ships, *Arahura*, *Aratere* and *Kaitaki*, all of which carry both passengers and their vehicles. There are up to 11 sailings each day so you should easily find one to suit your programme.

Once you're on board there are plenty of ways to pass the time when you're not admiring the view from one of the observation decks. If you're on the *Arahura*, meaning 'pathway to dawn', you can refresh yourself in the bar or food court or watch a movie — yep, there's even a cinema on

> Now you can see what your geography teacher meant by 'drowned valleys' . . .

Whichever ferry you're on, you can be sure of plenty of onboard entertainment while crossing Cook Strait.

board along with a private lounge, Club Class — which for a few extra dollars will separate you from the crowds. The *Aratere* (meaning 'quick path') is one of the most modern, high-tech vessels operating in New Zealand waters. It offers a similar range of onboard activities and facilities as well as a video games for children of all ages, live music and good coffee. Then there's the

Kaitaki (meaning 'challenger'); not only the largest ferry in the fleet but also in New Zealand, it can carry up to 1600 passengers. If you've got the kids with you, take advantage of the nurseries, play areas and — during school holidays and peak seasons — magicians and clowns as part of the onboard entertainment.

Island of glowing skies

You'll find Stewart Island, New Zealand's third-largest island, about 30 km south of the South Island, across Foveaux Strait. Around 85 per cent of the island is taken up by the 157,000 ha Rakiura National Park established in 2002 (Rakiura is Maori for 'the land of glowing skies', which was probably inspired by the night-time displays of aurora australis, the Southern Lights).

Let's be clear: you don't come to this far-flung place, with its permanent population of less than 500, in search of lots of social activity (although the pub in the island's one and only town of Oban can get quite lively). It's the outdoor stuff that draws visitors, so come prepared to spend your weekend on a combination of wilderness hiking, cycling, bird watching, fishing, diving or an organised cruise. Oh, and depending on the time of year, you may even get to try titi (also known as muttonbird), one of the local delicacies.

Bird watchers will revel in the sight of weka, kaka and tui that abound here; rumour has it kiwi are not too difficult to find, either — although your chances improve quite dramatically at night. All known kakapo have been transferred to various sanctuaries but

Peace and beauty await those hardy souls who cross Foveaux Strait to Stewart Island.

Expect to share your picnic lunch with some curious — and hungry — locals, such as this kaka.

it's possible that a few remain in the more remote parts of the island.

Keen walkers can choose between a three-day hike and shorter walks (some are not much more than a stroll while others will take up a whole morning or afternoon and require a moderate level of fitness). Although the DOC-managed tracks are mostly well formed and clearly sign-posted, do equip yourself with some decent walking shoes or boots plus protective clothing — the weather can change quickly and it can get very cold and wet. Choosing the longer option — the Rakiura Track, one of New Zealand's Great Walks — means you're in for a 36 km hike through lush native forest, plus lots of coastal beauty, amazing wildlife and a historic insight into the island.

If you're not in the mood for a long walk, hire a scooter and go exploring.

Some like it hot

A spontaneous visit in your own boat to White Island, 49 km off the coast of Whakatane, is not possible for reasons that will soon become clear — but if you're anywhere near this part of the east coast for a weekend, you can still get up close and personal with the country's only active marine volcano.

Captain James Cook dubbed it White Island back in 1769 because, according to his log book, ' as such it always appear'd to us'. However, its Maori name is Whakaari, meaning 'that which can be made visible' — most likely a reference to its tendency to disappear from sight on hazy days, only to reappear sharply on the horizon on clear ones. Back in Cook's time, Maori were regular visitors to the island, collecting sulphur to take back and put on their gardens on the mainland as well as muttonbirds and assorted fish that they'd cook in the steam jets issuing from the craters.

Because of the risks associated with its volcanic activity, only a limited number of tour operators is permitted to take visitors to the island, and in summer, when it becomes a very popular daytrip, it pays to book well ahead. All visitors are kitted out with safety gear including gas masks and hard hats, and you'll need to wear enclosed shoes (keep those high-heeled sandals for a night out in one of Whakatane's bars or cafes!).

The boat trip over to White Island takes just under an hour and a half, during which time you can spot dolphins, whales or — closer to the island — fur seals. On arrival a guide will lead you around the various sights. The highlights include the main crater, where the smell of sulphur and the hissing, roaring, eerie steam rising from the crater lake will have you suitably impressed, and further down the bright yellow chimneys of delicate sulphur crystals.

It's an exciting outing, that's for sure — and if you fancy looking down on it all from above, you can also visit the island by helicopter (an option that could make economic sense if there's a group of you).

Noxious fumes are all part of the experience; fortunately gas masks are part of the deal when you visit White Island.

Captain Cook called the island White
because cloud was all he could see.

The Queen's walkway

There are many good reasons to visit the stunningly scenic Marlborough Sounds but high on the list has to be the opportunity to walk the 71 km Queen Charlotte Track. The whole track stretching from historic Ship Cove to Anakiwa can be walked in as few as three days but if time and the boss allow, extend your holiday so you can take full advantage of this glorious experience. (Alternatively, you can join the track at a point of your choosing along the way and make it a shorter walk. Between March and November you can also hop on your mountain bike and cover it at speed!)

It's a spectacular track that offers the opportunity to engage in lots of enjoyable activities, including swimming, fishing, sailing, sea kayaking, mountain biking, bird watching and diving. There are also some interesting side trips, most taking around half a day, which are worth making a detour to see.

As with many of the longer walks, you can make this an entirely DIY experience and carry everything you'll need for the duration, or make arrangements with one of a number of operators to have your gear transported to various points. In any case, you can purchase a variety of goodies along the way. As for accommodation, there's something to suit everyone, ranging from campsites to luxury lodges.

If you go at a relatively quiet time of year, you may have some unexpected company — wild pigs have occasionally been spotted along the track rooting for food, especially on the section between Camp Bay and Torea Saddle. However, they won't harm you; in fact they are rather shy and will probably run a mile as soon as they notice you.

You'll need to be reasonably fit to enjoy the track, and as with any activity that takes you into the great outdoors you will have a much better time if you are properly prepared: there's heaps of valuable information on the DOC website (see page 236), so there's no excuse for cutting corners. Just remember not to leave rubbish anywhere on the track; all the more reason for not taking too much with you.

When time is not on your side, you can do the track at speed on a mountain bike.

Golden bays and green hillsides greet walkers on the Queen Charlotte Track.

You don't even have to carry your gear — it can be portaged by water taxi.

Castle Rock, Canterbury

ACTIVE ADVENTURES

Underwater utopia

Fancy a spot of exploration below the surface for a change? Well, head north and get yourself on a good-sized boat that's pointed towards the Poor Knights. This group of islands, possibly named after a bread-based pudding popular at the time of discovery by Europeans, is about 50 km northeast of Whangarei.

Unless you've got a special permit and scientific reasons to land or even tie up once you get there, you're not allowed to land. This is because the islands lie within the Poor Knights Marine Reserve, which was established back in 1981, and this status also prohibits disturbing marine life or removing any rocks or shells. It also means fishing is a big no-no; the point of visiting these islands is to go snorkelling or diving. And what a fabulous spot to do so — the Poor Knights feature in just about every major dive guide ever published and even if you don't end up getting in the water, you can learn an awful lot from the well-run, regular cruises in the area. Comprising two large islands with a group of smaller islets between them, the Poor Knights are the remnants of an ancient string of volcanoes and feature vast sea caves, tunnels and archways beneath the surface.

Quite a few charter boats operate from Tutukaka, north of Whangarei. Those that focus entirely on diving will be unsuitable unless you are a reasonably experienced scuba diver, while others gear the

experience towards the novice snorkeller and everyone in between, including those with a penchant for underwater photography. There are more than 100 fish species present — the sea around the islands having become a nursery for sub-tropical fish species — not to mention the wildly colourful range of sponges, anemones, sea urchins, nudibranchs, kelp and seaweed; so there's enough here for more than a few slide evenings to entertain the folks back home.

'Do you come here often?' A diver comes face to face with an inhabitant of the Poor Knights.

You wouldn't want to get between a shoal of determined maomao and their lunch!

Colourful wonders await the undersea visitor.

Climbing rocks!

Climbers work as a team at Castle Rock in Canterbury.

There are those among us with a better than average head for heights who spend their weekends having lots of fun rock climbing and 'bouldering'. If you're one of them, or considering becoming one, you should know about Wharepapa, which is a bit over two hours' drive south of Auckland.

A year-round destination, Wharepapa is a great place to climb even when it's been wet: the ignimbrite rock (volcanic material that was so hot its fragments welded together) dries quickly enabling you to get onto those steep and overhanging routes almost immediately after a bit of rain.

Apart from the 800 climbing routes over this most excellent set of rocks, Wharepapa is also popular because it boasts a store that stocks a good range of climbing equipment. It's also easy to find reasonable accommodation nearby so you can make the most of your weekend.

A top spot for bouldering is the South Island's Castle Hill, considered to be among New Zealand's best bouldering locations due to its thousands of amazing limestone rocks. With five climbing areas and only around an hour's drive from Christchurch, Castle Hill offers enough challenges to more than fill a weekend.

With a number of indoor walls now available in many of New Zealand's main and provincial centres, rock climbing doesn't have to be particularly weather dependent. In other words, if it's snowing

If it's raining, climb the walls at a facility such as the Christchurch YMCA.

or sleeting outside — or maybe just too hot to even consider putting on all that gear — climbers can head to the nearest indoor wall and get it out of their system without having to drive any great distance.

And just in case you think you can slide into any old clobber and grab a length of clothesline before tackling the rock of your choice, think again. You really do need to spend some money on good-quality equipment. It's a bit like choosing car tyres — they are all that's between you and a very hard surface!

Feel the fear and . . .

This is where it all started for AJ Hackett and his entrepreneurial mates: the Kawarau Gorge, near Queenstown.

Ever since entrepreneurs AJ Hackett and Henry van Asch set up the first commercial bungy jump in New Zealand, adrenalin junkies have been lining up to experience this adventure sport for themselves. The jumps, usually based on a platform or bridge, tend to range in height from 35 to 134 m (or 192 m in the case of Auckland's Sky Tower jump).

So where in New Zealand can you go for your share of the action? The aforementioned Sky Tower Sky Jump is a cable-controlled base jump that has you leaping feet or head first 192 m from the tower's outdoor observation deck, wearing a special suit with a full body harness attached to a wire cable. Once you're over that rush, move on to the Auckland Harbour Bridge bungy, where you'll be taken to a state-of-the-art jump pod to leap 40 m to sea level before being winched back up.

Further south there's more bungy jumping in both Rotorua (43 m above the Ngongotaha River at the Agrodome agricultural theme park, which offers heaps of activities so there's plenty to do before and after you jump) and Taupo (from a platform where your friends can watch you leap 47 m down to the Waikato River below). Still in the North Island, the Mokai Gravity Canyon near Taihape (80 m) offers day and night jumps and tandem swings.

Moving on to the South Island, if you're a novice you might want to do your first

Auckland's Harbour Bridge bungy provides a new angle on the city.

jump at Thrillseeker's Canyon Bungy on the 135-year-old Waiau Ferry Bridge near Hanmer Springs (at a mere 35 m it's the lowest of all the bungy sites).

Mount Hutt Bungy's claim to fame is that it's the highest-altitude jump in New Zealand, while still further south is the 100-year-old Kawarau suspension bridge, the world's first dedicated bungy jump site.

There are three other bungy jump sites in the Queenstown area: the Queenstown Ledge Bungy (where you take a running jump to launch yourself 400 m above Queenstown) plus the Bungy Sky Swing — a night swing where it's advised you eat afterwards; Skipper's Canyon (71 m high and only available to groups); and Nevis Highwire (at 134 m the highest jump down into a canyon, whose walls narrow dramatically as you get closer to the water).

Rolling on the rivers

The *Waipa Delta* is soon to relocate to Auckland, where she will roll on the harbour.

You might not be old enough to be word perfect in — or even to have heard of — Creedence Clearwater Revival's late 1960s song 'Proud Mary', but for the record it's all about being on a paddle steamer. Here in New Zealand you can have your own paddle steamer adventure, albeit at a fairly sedate pace, on board the PS *Waimarie*. Designed in London in 1899 and shipped to Wanganui in kitset form, this vessel — originally named *Aotea* — plied the Whanganui River along with nearly a dozen other similar craft for many years, carrying cargo and mail and catering to tourists keen to experience the novelty of such a voyage.

As roading improved in the region, the riverboats were used less and less and the *Waimarie* came to a somewhat ignominious end when, several years after being taken out of service, she was allowed to sink at her berth.

Salvaged in 1993 by a group of volunteers, the old boat gradually gained a new lease on life as restoration work got under way. In early 2000, after years of work including the rebuilding of her hull, the restored *Waimarie* was proudly recommissioned for her new life on the Whanganui River as the country's only authentic paddle steamer. In her first year of operation, PS *Waimarie* carried over 25,000 passengers.

Now the only paddle steamer on

![Waimarie paddle steamer on the river]

Considering the *Waimarie* is soon to celebrate her 110th birthday, she's looking pretty good.

the river, *Waimarie* offers daily trips all year round (except in August) with her comfortably equipped saloons, covered and open sun decks, refreshments and a licensed bar, commentary and working steam engines on view.

In Hamilton, locals and visitors alike have for the last 25 years enjoyed the presence of the *Waipa Delta*, a replica paddle steamer that has been a popular venue for a wide variety of events as well as regular trips down the river. It was a relaxing way to see the river areas of central Hamilton, but as of late 2009 the *Waipa Delta* will be based at the National Maritime Museum in Auckland.

No barrier to adventure

Much of the appeal in a visit to the Barrier — as it's fondly known to residents of the Hauraki Gulf — is what you can't do there. The island's official tourism website proudly lists the lack of modern facilities, so when you're ready for a weekend in a place where the locals thrive for precisely that reason, pack your bags and head for the Barrier.

Great Barrier Island is a 30-minute plane trip or a two and a half hour ferry trip from Auckland. It's a substantial chunk of land, much of which is covered in slowly regenerating forest. Some very heavy duty logging and milling took place here during the nineteenth century, as well as copper, gold and silver mining. All this left its mark, not necessarily in the most scenic way.

But the forest is looking much healthier these days, especially now that vigilant pest control has eradicated most threats. You can look forward to the bliss of natural hot springs, waterfalls and swimming holes, all far from the madding crowd. The coastline is for the most part pristine, too — featuring white-sand ocean beaches on the east side with more sheltered spots on the west coast. Note that locals are always grateful to find volunteers willing to help clean up the coastline after the heavy marine traffic of summer.

Be sure to pack for the outdoors when you plan a weekend here — over 20 tracks and trails await you, and good old DOC has put together a great trampers' map with an easy-to-follow track-number system plus relevant information for each walk. If you're worried about where to leave your rental car, you can arrange a drop-off and pick-up service.

Mountain biking is also a great way of exploring the island, and the trails offer plenty of variety; they vary in difficulty from non-challenging climbs through bush and farm land to fast downhills and technical climbs. Kayaking allows you to enjoy the coastline, especially the western shoreline with its sheltered coves and inlets.

Why not bring your golf clubs? If the nine-hole golf course is not open, visitors with their own clubs are welcome to use the honesty box.

The pristine sands on the Barrier's eastern side, such as these at Medlands Beach, are a great drawcard for visitors.

Not far to go to the bar after the thirsty work
of rowing ashore . . .

Uphill and . . . up more hills!

When you really want to stretch yourself beyond your normal fitness regime, the Kepler Challenge and its sister event, the Luxmore Grunt, will determine whether or not you're iron man material. Established as a way to support community projects in Fiordland, this annual Kepler Track event, which has been held on the first Saturday in December since 1988, challenges runners of all abilities through its 60 km mountain run and 27 km Luxmore Grunt mountain 'grind' (thus named with very good reason).

Because of the potential to damage the surroundings, the Kepler Challenge is limited to 400 competitors and the Grunt to just 150. If you're in good shape you should be able to complete the entire course in somewhere between 5 and 11 hours (the current record is 4:37:41 in the men's race and 05:23:34 in the women's!).

Starting at the control gates of Lake Te Anau, the route follows an easy 6 km before climbing steadily up to the Luxmore Hut. The next 12 km take runners along

The views from the Luxmore Hut are stunning — if you stop and take a breath during the Luxmore Grunt.

Heavenly views provide extra inspiration on the Kepler Challenge.

the undulating tops (great views!) before a spectacular descent to the Iris Burn Hut. A gradual 17 km journey down the Iris Burn, a glacial valley, brings competitors to the Moturau Hut on Lake Manapouri and from there it's a 6 km run to the last checkpoint at Rainbow Reach. The home straight follows the Waiau River and back to the control gates. The concurrent Luxmore Grunt event follows the same route as far as the Luxmore Hut, then returns via the same route back to the control gates.

The community-based event is made possible by lots of local volunteers, who operate the checkpoints, and provide communications, first aid and other services. It attracts people from all over so don't be surprised to find keen runners from far-flung corners of the world hot on your heels.

For those who want to know exactly what they're in for, 15.7 km of the track is uphill and 22 km is downhill.

There are heaps of prizes, including cash and assistance to the next event for the first finishers. All competitors receive a commemorative medal on finishing and a certificate of achievement as souvenirs of the event. Go on — register your entry now!

Watery thrills and spills

Some people just love to feel the adrenalin coursing through their veins and white water rafting is definitely a way to get this happening — fast! However, it's not a loner sport so you'll need to head away for a weekend with a group or take your chances and see who else fronts up on the day. The trips vary in length from an experimental 45 minutes up to several days of full-on adventure.

Rivers where this kind of rafting takes place are graded from 1 through to 5: grades 1–2 are suitable for novices and families; grades 3–4 involve much bigger waves, stronger currents and obstacles to manoeuvre around; while grade 5 features even stronger currents, bigger waves, boulders and holes — features that could hole and flip boats. There is also a grade 6, which the New Zealand Rafting Association describes as 'extremely difficult to successfully manoeuvre due to significantly steeper vertical drops and boulders. Usually considered unrunnable'. Trained raft guides are mandatory for any trips rated 3 or higher, but whatever grade you undertake you can expect a pretty thorough briefing covering safety and related matters before you set out for your adventure.

North Island rivers where white water rafting is popular include the Wairoa (5), Kaituna (5), Rangitaiki (3–4), Motu (3–4), Tongariro (2–3) and Rangitikei (2–5). Rafting can also be enjoyed on the Otaki (2–3) and

No, that raft did not just come down that waterfall!

Hutt (3) rivers.

In the upper South Island you could spend weeks checking out all the rivers and still not have tried them all, but here's a list to help you decide: Karamea (5), Buller (2–4), Grey (4), Hokitika (3–4), Clarence (2–3), Arnold (2), Perth (5), Whataroa (5), Landsborough (3–5), Waiatoto (4), Arahura (4–5), Whanganui (yes, there's one in the South Island, too, and it's graded 3–4) and Taipo (3). And don't overlook the Kawarau

**Paddlers get wet — and love it — on
Canterbury's Rangitata River.**

(3–4) or Shotover (3–5) rivers further south near Queenstown. Last but not least for serious adrenalin junkies is a heli-rafting experience, which involves a helicopter flight to raft launch sites that are usually inaccessible by road.

When you book your trip, it always pays to check what kind of equipment is standard but generally you can expect to be provided with (at the very least) a hard hat, wetsuit, booties and lifejacket and, of course, a paddle. If you decide to go rafting during the colder months, you'll also be provided with neoprene socks, mittens or gloves, and a lightweight thermal top.

Surf's up

It's amazing when you consider the age range and lifestyles of surfers these days — they come in all shapes and sizes from teenage thrill seekers to middle-aged business types. Government sports agency SPARC estimates that more than 200,000 New Zealanders surf, so if you haven't already given it a go, get yourself some gear or even better sign up at a surf school (there are more than a dozen in the North Island and three in the South Island): discover for yourself the thrill of being out there on a big wave.

Northland is a surfer's dream that makes for some excellent beach breaks with its big swells on the west coast and easterly winds on the other side. Auckland-based surfers can have a wild time anywhere from Whatipu to Muriwai, but they need to watch out for the powerful rips, which are best avoided by novices.

The surf breaks south of Raglan are famous in the southern hemisphere (the area appeared in the 1966 cult surfing movie *Endless Summer*), and Whangamata and Waihi on the opposite coast attract thousands over the summer months. The long ocean swells coming from both the east and south are a feature that makes Gisborne's beaches popular among surfers — and for experienced board riders there's nothing like the thrill of remote wilderness surfing off the Mahia Peninsula. Taranaki's Oakura and Opunake beaches both offer

A surfer at sundown on Piha Beach, west of Auckland.

A surfer hits the lip in big surf off the Taranaki coast.

some challenging action and there's also some heavy surf to be found on the rugged Wairarapa coast.

A surfing experience on the Mainland has to include Kaikoura, where you may even spot a passing pod of dolphins or find yourself under the supervision of fur seals. Everything from tame breakers through to heavy rollers can be found further south, and in some bays on the Otago Peninsula, southerly winds off the iceshelf create perfectly formed tunnel waves. Over on the West Coast there's plenty of surfing action on what is hailed as the wildest stretch of exposed surf coastline in New Zealand.

As with many outdoor sports, you can surf summer or winter but you'll need to make an investment in a good wetsuit and accessories (think neoprene) — for obvious reasons.

Sports central

The great expanse of Lake Taupo and its surrounds make for an impressive variety of adventure activities, not least of which is bungy jumping (see page 112); however, you might consider starting your weekend instead with a tandem skydive — what better way to see the whole area and decide which bits will be worth further investigation?

Once you're back on terra firma, book yourself a few hours of fun on a quad bike (you don't need experience, and helmets are provided). Quad-bike tours will take you over special-terrain trails through gorgeous bush with tantalising views along the way.

Fancy a spot of abseiling? You're in the right place given the variety of rocks and mountains within a bull's roar. Indoor climbing is also on the menu; one of New Zealand's largest climbing walls, with graded climbs and qualified instructors at hand, can be found in Taupo.

And the lake itself? At more than 160 m deep, it's the largest body of fresh water in Australasia. Choose from a huge range of adrenalin-fuelled activities including (but not limited to) parasailing, wakeboarding, waterskiing, diving, speedboating and jetskiing.

Further water-related fun — for example kayaking, rafting, or jetboating — can be had in and around the local rivers including the Tongariro, Waikato or Tokaanu. Then there's the fishing . . . what could beat the thrill of landing and, later on, eating a good-sized trout?

Keen hunters will find plenty of targets in this region: deer, goat, turkey and wild pig can all be found around the mountains, forests and scrublands. Get there via four-wheel-drive or organise yourself a helicopter if you want a true wilderness experience.

Remember too that Taupo is close to some premier snowfields where you can ski and snowboard to your heart's content. After all this activity, you're going to need a soak in a soothing hot pool — take your pick!

Skysurfing gives you thrills and, as in this case, the best view.

Kayakers admire the giant Maori carvings at Mine Bay in Taupo's western bays.

101 MUST-DO WEEKENDS AA

From ghost to ghost

A sporting event that suits different levels of fitness has to be a good thing, but when it has the added attraction of being held in the stunning region of Central Otago — specifically in the historic mining town of St Bathans —it's practically compulsory. This one has been going since 1989 and all money raised as a result goes towards the St Bathans and Becks communities for environmental projects (another good thing!).

The St Bathans Ghost to Ghost Triathlon is named after a non-paying long-term guest who, so the story goes, resides in ectoplasmic form in the town's historic Vulcan Hotel, built during the town's goldrush and nowadays the triathlon's starting point.

Each March several hundred people gather here under the benign summer skies and sort themselves into one of two categories: masters — which covers men aged 50 and over plus women aged 45 and over — and then everyone else! The triathlon starts with a 250 m dash from the Vulcan to the Blue Lake. There contestants must canoe two circuits of what was once a huge pit that, after years of mining activity, was allowed to fill. They then run back up the hill to the Vulcan, where they jump on a mountain bike before tackling a 14 km trail that takes them out of town, up the hill below the Blue Lake, down to Grey Lake, through gold dredgings and a pine plantation, with an extra loop of the upper road back to the Vulcan.

The third and final leg comprises a 7 km run uphill out of town, along the ridge overlooking the Blue Lake, then down and around the Grey Lake, onto a four-wheel-drive vehicle track through the pine plantation, onto the main road and finally back to the Vulcan.

If all this sounds a tad energetic for your group, then maybe the duathlon held on the same day is the way to go.

Running, canoeing, cycling and then more running before you're allowed a beer.

It all finishes up here, at the Vulcan Hotel in St Bathans, where you could be served (or observed) by the resident ghost.

Polynesian Spa, Rotorua

RELAX &
INDULGE

Pack the rod and clubs

The good old 'mates' weekend' still has an important place in Kiwi culture, and when the mood strikes, there's nothing better for a bloke than taking time out to bond with others in the local tribe. It's a big improvement on moping around the house!

Two of the most popular bonding activities would have to be golfing and fishing. When it comes to the latter there are plenty of places in New Zealand where a bunch of blokes — or good keen women — can spend a day happily getting cold and wet while attempting to outsmart a river or lake full of crafty fish who've seen it all before.

Whether you prefer sea or fresh water fishing, it's a great weekend away for the boys.

Golf is another great way to relax and bond.

If heading for a river or lake is the plan, then you'll probably be after trout, in which case you'll need a licence. Conditions and seasons vary from region to region so it's best to check on the Fish and Game website (www.fishandgame.org.nz) well before setting off. The lure of a fishing trip on the deep blue sea generally comes without such bureaucratic strings apart from rules on fish size and catch limits, but make sure common sense plays its part regarding lifejackets and emergency equipment.

Once the fish has been filleted, put on ice or whatever cunning plan you have in place to get your catch home in the best possible shape, it's time to play a round or nine — or even 18. You needn't look too far to find a golf course — it's been estimated you don't have to drive more than 45 minutes anywhere in New Zealand to find one. There you'll no doubt have a great time, as often as not working up to a well-deserved spell at the 19th hole.

You and your mates can decide between an immaculately manicured resort-style course (see page 136) or perhaps one that's rather more rustically rural — all up, there are more than 400 of them to choose from.

Live it up at a lodge

No pesky neighbours in sight — or even on site — at Huka Lodge, near Taupo.

Go on, you only live once! Treat yourself to an extravagant weekend at one of the country's luxury lodges and find out why well-heeled international travellers go out of their way for a very special touch of Kiwi-style lotus-eating.

One of the first luxury lodges to establish itself on the local scene was Huka Lodge, set on the scenic banks of the Waikato River in the central North Island. People continue to come here for all sorts of reasons; maybe a romantic weekend or perhaps a group experience or just a 'get away from it all' couple of days (royalty has been spotted doing just this on more than one occasion). The main lodge, known as the Lodge Room, is exquisitely appointed, making it the most wonderful haven at which to gather over a late afternoon or evening aperitif. Each of the 20 secluded but spacious guest suites is beautifully fitted out and has its own outdoor terrace, from which guests may well hear the 'plop' of a rising trout from the nearby river. As you would expect, fine dining is the order of the day, accompanied by great wines; such is the size of the wine cellar, with its vaulted ceilings, that it serves as a magnificent dining room in its own right.

Down in the South Island the location of award-winning Blanket Bay Lodge on the bush-clad shores of Lake Wakatipu, just 40 km from Queenstown, is equally if not more magnificent. Three dining rooms, each with

> Choosing between the three dining rooms at Blanket Bay Lodge might be the hardest decision you make here.

an enormous log-burning fireplace, offer a choice of Pacific Rim cuisine that will have you salivating before you've even opened the wine list.

Listed among the top resort hideaways in the world, the lodge offers every comfort you can think of, including super king-size beds in which to loll about in your lakeside room or suite, your own private sitting area, a bathroom fitted with every luxurious touch . . . You'll never want to leave — especially once you've enjoyed some of the exclusive facilities that are available to guests, including a swimming pool, steam rooms, fully equipped gym and games room. By the way, don't worry about over-crowding — Blanket Bay Lodge has just five guest rooms and five suites.

Cool wine and warm water

There's wine — and farmers' markets — in them there valleys!

Although wine is a relatively new industry in Canterbury's Waipara Valley it hasn't taken long for the area to catch up with the other major wine-growing regions and at last count there were around 80 vineyards, with more planned. Basing yourself here for a weekend will more than satisfy your oenophilic tendencies (i.e. having a serious interest in wine, for those who haven't come across this impressive word before).

There are also plenty of related activities over the summer months, including a great farmers' market showcasing local produce — lamb, vegetables, olive oils, eggs, honey, preserves, bread and more from growers between the Waimakariri and Conway

People have been soaking in the waters of
Hanmer Springs for nearly 125 years.

rivers. Be sure to bring your own shopping bag — the market is a minimal plastic zone. If possible, plan your weekend to coincide with the annual Waipara Wine and Food Celebration that takes place in early March.

Not much more than an hour's drive northwest is the spa town of Hanmer Springs, where, you guessed it, you can soak away all your troubles in one of nine open-air thermal pools, three sulphur pools, and four private thermal pools. There's also a sauna/steam room in which to start or finish your ablutions.

Folk have been enjoying these geothermal waters, which range in temperature between 33 and 42 degrees Celsius, for the last 125 years; initially the water was under artesian pressure but today it is pumped from a bore.

It's hard to imagine having enough of this kind of treat but should the urge to get more physical overtake you, there are plenty of outdoor activities to choose from whatever time of year you're here: a game of golf, a hike through the forest or a mountain bike ride are just a few. During winter, of course, you're just an hour away from two fantastic skifields.

Tee off at a resort course

Now and again it's fun to dust off the clubs, pack your best bib and tucker and book a weekend in one of New Zealand's idyllic golf resorts. Purpose-built and designed so that visitors lack for nothing, these resorts offer a totally rejuvenating — and even hedonistic if you're that way inclined — weekend experience.

One of the most famous of these is Queenstown's Millbrook, an 18-hole championship golf course that can be enjoyed all year round. The accommodation is world class and there are enough facilities to keep guests happily occupied when they're not playing golf, but for those who want to explore the region, Central Otago has it all: vineyards, adventure sports, skifields, the list goes on . . .

Just 15 minutes' drive from Christchurch is the Clearwater Resort, a par 72 championship course designed by John Darby in consultation with Sir Bob Charles. As with all golf resorts of this calibre, special attention has been paid to make the outlook well beyond the ordinary —as you make your way around the course, you can enjoy a vista of spring-fed lakes and trout-filled streams framed by uninterrupted views of the Southern Alps. Here, the choice of accommodation ranges from well-appointed lakeside rooms and suites to spacious two-bedroom apartments with cosy fireplaces.

Never let it be said that the North Island

Practise your putting at your leisure surrounded by luxury.

Enjoy spectacular views with your round at Milbrook Golf Resort.

lacks its share of golf resorts — at last count there were seven, all of which offer superb facilities with fairways and greens set amid magnificent scenery. Carrington Golf Resort on Northland's Karikari Peninsula is one whose oceanside location, with spectacular views and rolling inland course, makes it a very popular destination for local and overseas visitors. Included in the price of your stay at Carrington is a scrumptious breakfast and a five-course dinner, the ingredients of which are for the most part locally sourced.

Unleash your inner artist

There's no shortage of reasons to visit the top of the South Island — after all, the weather and scenery are legendary — but how about spending a couple of days confirming why so many creative types flourish here? Did you know that the region has more 'working artists' per capita than anywhere else in the country? There are plenty of opportunities to meet them in their studios, galleries or workshops and, in some cases, using their premises and facilities to try your hand at creating your own art.

Options include learning to weave your own basket with harakeke (New Zealand flax); visiting a bead gallery where you can put together whatever combination of baubles you fancy; a few hours at a Japanese

Ceramic artist Katie Gold works in her studio at Upper Moutere, Nelson.

calligraphy school; or a workshop where you can create your very own bone-carving souvenir. These workshops tend to be quite informal, with an emphasis on having fun (which is, after all, a key ingredient for an enjoyable weekend).

If you're keen on working with wood, consider signing up for a short course in carving at the Centre for Fine Woodworking, the only one of its kind in New Zealand. They also offer courses for craft furniture makers.

One of the region's most popular attractions is the Höglund Art Glass Studio and Gallery, which is open all year round and offers weekend glass-blowing and bead-making workshops. Imagine how impressed your friends and relatives will be when you come home with such a creative variety of souvenirs, all made by your own fair hands.

Then of course there's all the stuff to look at while you're here. Remember that this is where WOW (World of Wearable Art) was born and even though this internationally famous annual event now takes place in Wellington, there is plenty to see — including winning entries — at the World of Wearable Art and Collectable Cars Museum.

And don't forget Nelson's markets. Over summer there are the Friday night Bayleys twilight art markets in Trafalgar Park and the adjoining Trafalgar Centre, and the Saturday morning market, with its many artistic offerings alongside all the yummy home-made or home-grown delicacies, will definitely help put you in a creative mood.

Glass artists also abound around Nelson.

Love is in the air

For nearly 20 years Christchurch was the place to be if you wanted to have a romantic weekend. Sadly, the Festival of Romance has now been removed from the official calendar but Christchurch still offers some great romantic experiences.

An excellent start for you and your loved one could be a special ride down the Avon in a custom built, beautifully upholstered punt with your very own boatman who'll guide you past the sights of the central city.

Once you've got a taste for being on the move, you might like to try a ride on a fully restored heritage tram, a unique way to wind your way through the heart of the city while the driver gives a friendly and informative commentary. Jump on and off at any of the 11 stops along the way; there'll be another tram along to pick you up a bit later and if you just can't bear the thought of eating dinner somewhere stationary, well, you don't have to . . . that's

There are few things more romantic — or spectacular — than a hot air balloon ride over the Canterbury Plains.

You can choose when to hop on or off this vintage tram during its circuit of central Christchurch.

right, there's even a restaurant tram so you can dine aboard while following the 2.5 km inner-city track.

Or how about a romantic hot air balloon ride? Just make sure you have an early night because you'll need to be up before the crack of dawn so that you're ready to take to the skies at sunrise. Imagine the glorious sensation of floating high above the city as the sun rises out of the ocean. You'll be able to see for miles and truly appreciate the vastness of the Canterbury Plains, not to mention the grandeur of the Southern Alps.

Finish off the weekend with a leisurely stroll through the city's picturesque and extensive Hagley Park. What you'll see will depend on the season; for example, spring offers acre upon acre of gorgeous daffodils, while later in the year the paths will be covered in great drifts of multi-hued autumn leaves through which to crunch your way. You might even be lucky enough to come across a crop of the famously elusive porcini mushrooms rumoured to grow in certain parts of the park.

Primp and pamper

Every woman knows that getaway weekends are an essential part of female friendships and they come highly recommended. Sometimes they're about shopping (see page 146), sometimes they're about getting right away from it all and sometimes they're about sheer indulgence. When it's time for the latter, why would you go past a day spa at one of New Zealand's specialist resorts?

In the North Island, Rotorua is bursting with ways to pamper you and your friends — and multi-sensory spa treatments including balneotherapy (otherwise known as bath therapy) are the order of the day. In this part of the country, mud features in many of the treatments; think mud baths, mud packs and mud wraps. It's not any old mud, either, but thermal mud, which is known to contain rich minerals that will leave your skin glowing. Steam also plays a role in the rejuvenation process, as do a variety of massages ranging from the purely relaxing to those that involve placing heated rocks on certain parts of the body. There are a number of detox options, too, that will leave you squeaky clean inside and out.

The South Island alpine resort village of Hanmer Springs has world-class spa facilities where just about every part of your body can benefit. Here you can book yourself in for almost any kind of massage you can think of, including specialist Vichy massage treatments, deep tissue and relaxation massages, and detoxifying body wraps, facials, pedicures and manicures. Those hankering for a mud treatment won't be disappointed, either — the healing properties of Rotorua's thermal mud are also recognised down here and so the magical brown stuff is brought in accordingly. Don't forget to spend some time in the soothing geothermal waters before or after your spa treatment; it will distract you in the best way possible so you'll emerge relaxed and ready to face the world again.

As every woman knows, these indulgences don't come cheap — but a few hours' investment in being kind to yourself can pay off for the weeks and months to come.

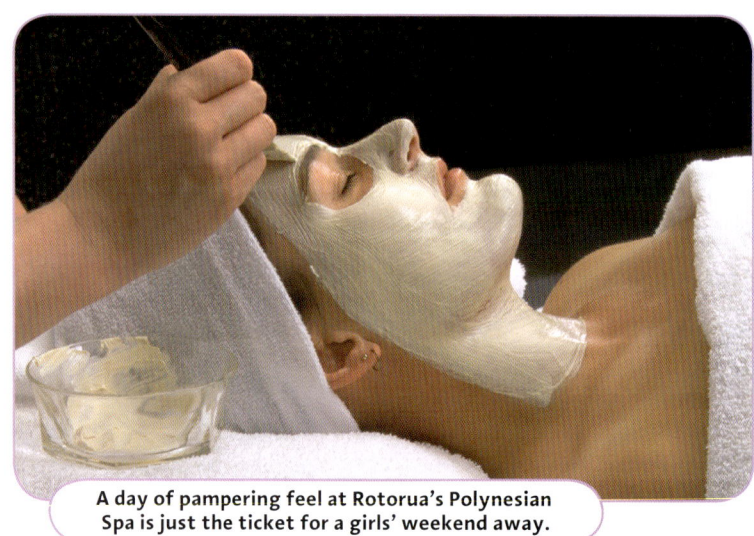

A day of pampering feel at Rotorua's Polynesian Spa is just the ticket for a girls' weekend away.

Have a soak and a gossip in Rotorua or Hanmer Springs (inset).

Capital café culture

A sunny day brings locals and visitors out in droves to Wellington's Cuba Mall.

A weekend spent in the capital would not be complete without a good dose of people watching — and what better place to indulge this harmless hobby than in some of Wellington's famous cafés. For those of you who thought a café was merely a place to pop in for a brief bout of refreshment, it's time to think again.

Since the sixties, Wellington has been famous for colourful cafés that are renowned as much for their regulars as for their more obvious attractions. The most well known of these was probably Suzy's, where anyone with an aspiration to be someone used to congregate. These days Suzy's is but a fond memory, although many establishments have survived an impressive number of years. Visiting these cafés is about more than just a caffeine boost, however: the city also abounds in modern cafés, and such is their quality it seems unfair to single out any by name. A much better way to discover this buzzy city's café culture would be to focus on a particular part of town, and wander around it until a particular combination of sights, sounds and smells lures you in.

Cuba Street and its immediate environs boast enough cafés to keep you enthralled for the whole weekend. Here you'll not only find a fabulous mix of sophistication and seediness, but also a wonderful ethnic mix. If the need for fresh air arises, drag yourself away and head down to the waterfront where you can sit in comfort over your coffee and admire the view as well as all those business types striding purposefully past. Then there's Newtown, just a quick ride on a big yellow trolley bus from the city centre. Still largely ungentrified, this colourful part of Wellington could have you choosing a Turkish coffee rather than your usual flat white.

Whatever your tipple, you can count on getting much more out of it than just a quick caffeine fix when you drink it in Wellington.

You can't beat Wellington on a good day, catching up at the Chocolate Fish Café in Scorching Bay.

Shop till you drop

Auckland's Chancery is a shopper's paradise, with a mixture of local and international brands.

Besides pampering yourself at a spa (see page 142), few things compare to a good dose of retail therapy in an area chock full of wickedly delicious shops when you want to feel good about yourself.

In Christchurch, it's pretty hard to go past Ballantyne's for a good spend-up. This reputable department store has been catering to Canterbury's landed gentry — and everyone else who might be shopping for a special something — since 1854. The number of departments (from fabulous clothes to fine china and just about everything in between) is indeed impressive and this makes it decadently easy to spend the best part of a day exploring them. There's not only a great range of goodies to choose from, but you'll also enjoy the kind of service that just simply doesn't exist in most other places.

Arriving in Wellington with a well-loaded credit card is also a pleasure and one of your first stops should be Kirkcaldie & Stains, the city's most prestigious department store, affectionately known as Kirks. Kirks' history goes back as far as 1863 and, like Ballantyne's, it stocks a wonderful range of quality merchandise presented by courteous and knowledgeable staff. If time allows, you should also visit Moore Wilson's recently renovated premises. Their range of fresh produce is second to none and you can also pick up everything you can think of that has some kind of kitchen connection.

Dunedin also has some great shopping, in heritage buildings.

Up in Auckland, you're in serious mall territory but fear not — the Queen City boasts its own classy department store, Smith & Caughey, located in downtown Queen Street. Unfortunately its legendary tearooms no longer exist, but the café is not too bad. Then there's the fantastic shopping precinct in Newmarket where the label conscious can shop until their cards run dry (perish the thought!). Think Saks, Hugo Boss, Karen Walker, Kate Sylvester, Trelise Cooper — and that's just for starters.

The heart of art

When you find yourself up in the Far North following the Hokianga 'Heart Trail', you'll come across a host of artistic treats, many of which are made from local natural resources and are available for purchase. The trail connects the north and south sides of the Hokianga Harbour and has been planned to provide a wonderfully scenic trip that involves calling in to various working studios, galleries and workshops to see — and perhaps buy — art work. All artists associated with the trail will welcome your visit, but in nearly all cases you'll need to phone first to make an appointment.

Close to 25 listed artists, artisans, art galleries, craft shops, design stores and outlets make up the trail, which stretches from the Waipoua Forest to Rawene, across the harbour and then northwards. The arts and crafts on offer comprise landscape and contemporary painting, photography, prints, found items, wood carvings, jewellery, glass work, pottery, sculpture and weaving including handwoven kete (flax baskets). For those wanting their own artistic experience, several of the workshops offer tuition in specific subjects.

Along the way, stop and relax at one

Culture and cafés come together on the Hokianga Heart Trail.

101 MUST-DO WEEKENDS AA

The Boatshed Café in Rawene is on the trail.

of the recommended cafés or perhaps stay the night at a friendly bed and breakfast. Each of the available comfortable accommodation options has been chosen to complement the theme of the trail. And of course as you make your way north along this artistic adventure you'll experience the vehicular ferry connecting Rawene with the other side of the harbour.

You can get the free Heart Trail brochure, with all the relevant names, phone numbers and addresses, from information centres throughout this part of Northland, or check it out at www.hokiangatourism.co.nz.

Follow the hearts for an adventure for art lovers.

Tom McDonald Cellar, Church Road Winery, Hawke's Bay

FOOD & WINE

Dine among the vines

The very best place to enjoy the heavenly marriage between wine and food has to be in a vineyard restaurant where both components are locally produced.

When you combine this experience with a warm and sunny climate, there's some wonderful weekend eating to be had throughout New Zealand's wine regions.

Waiheke Island is one that springs to mind and whose romantic weekend getaway associations can only be enhanced by a lunch high up at Te Whau, overlooking the vines and the sparkling waters of the Hauraki Gulf beyond. North of Auckland are a number of vineyard cafés that vie to be the best — including the Oak Grill Bistro at Ascension, the restaurant at Heron's Flight in Matakana and Gracehill Café out west in Kumeu.

Hawke's Bay is another region where an

The Carrington Estate on the Karikari Peninsula, Northland, offers great winery dining.

Many of the vineyards in Hawke's Bay offer a bite to eat as well as a chance to taste.

al fresco vineyard dining experience will add something very special to a weekend away. The only problem will be deciding where to go, given the choice of establishments that specialise in making your lunch or dinner truly memorable. Among the best, however, are Sileni Estates, Craggy Range and Mission Estate. Further south in Martinborough the weather may not be quite so balmy but lunch at Murdoch James Winery Café is a warming experience in every sense of the word.

It's not possible to do justice here to the variety and high standards of vineyard cafés in the South Island but when the sun is shining, it's hard to beat a Marlborough vineyard; just imagine yourself drinking in the stunning view — and those golden drops — at either Highfield Estate or Herzog Winery and Restaurant. Waipara, in North Canterbury, is home to Pegasus Bay wines, whose picture-perfect vineyard, along with its restaurant, has long been a destination in itself. Meanwhile, Central Otago keeps raising the bar. Lunch at Gibbston Valley is hard to beat although Mt Difficulty, with its highly acclaimed pinot noir, comes pretty close.

Fresh food and friendly folk

Up in Whangarei they've known the value of a farmers' market for some time; in fact it was here that the country's first such market started back in 1997. Since then, the concept has taken New Zealand by storm and now a number of well-established markets run from one end of the country to the other. There vendors sell what they grow, farm, pickle, preserve, bake, smoke or catch themselves from within a defined local area.

The area just north of Auckland up to the Bay of Islands is particularly blessed with these markets; not least of which is the one that takes place in Kerikeri every Sunday from 8.30am to midday (with extended hours over summer). Expect to find lots of fresh produce including subtropical fruits and gourmet goods such as locally roasted coffee.

The Whangarei growers' market sets up its assorted stalls every Saturday morning

Partaking of the goodies on offer at the local farmers' market doesn't have to be restricted to food.

between 6.30am and 10.30am, so it pays to get there early. It's a fairly basic affair but the standard and range of produce is high.

Heading southwest, the Paparoa farmers' market on State Highway 12 has been in operation since 2007 and is held fortnightly on Saturdays from 9am to midday. Highlights here are the locally grown seasonal produce, fresh flounder, oysters, smoked mussels, pickles and sauces.

Possibly the best known farmers' market in this neck of the woods is the purpose-built establishment in the picturesque village of Matakana. It can get very crowded here during summer because of all the related activity such as live music, so it pays not to arrive too late. In summer the market operates every Saturday from 8am through to 1pm, while in winter it's all over at midday.

Closer to Auckland you'll find the Puhoi farmers' market, a relaxed affair on the last Sunday of every month between 8.30 am and 12.30pm. Whichever market you visit, consider stocking up for a picnic and heading off to the beach or perhaps a peaceful grassy reserve for a lazy lunch. There's certainly no shortage of perfect picnic spots in this part of New Zealand.

Buying your veggies from the Matakana farmer's market means knowing exactly where they come from.

Taste the good life

Fresh seasonal produce, tasty beef, succulent seafood, tangy oils and olives, and a choice of the country's best wine; have you died and gone to heaven? No, you're in Hawke's Bay, a region where they are so proud of what they produce that in 2000 they developed a food trail that will have you salivating before you've even set off. So go easy on breakfast, clean out the chilly bin, arm yourself with the specially designed food trail map — freely available at hotels, i-SITES, etc. —and prepare to give your tastebuds a treat.

The Hawke's Bay food trail, with its 85 food-related stops, stretches from Mahia to Norsewood and features just about every epicurean delight you can think of. These include, but are not limited to, seasonal treats such as asparagus and strawberries, gourmet meats and small goods, game and

seafood, olive products, verjuice, honey, eggs, cheese and chocolate. Each food trail destination is well marked at the gate or entrance, with a corresponding number on the food trail map, so you'll have no trouble spotting participating outlets and businesses.

All these wonderful treats are made possible thanks to the region's benevolent climate and fertile plains — and we haven't even begun to touch on the wine, oh the wine . . . Some of New Zealand's big boys in the wine industry have been operating here for years (for instance, Corbans, Craggy Range, etc.) but there are also quite a few boutique vineyards that offer cellar door facilities.

Last but not least, Hawke's Bay is also home to some of the country's best farmers' markets: there's the market in Napier on Tennyson Street every Saturday morning and again at the Hawke's Bay Showgrounds on Sunday mornings, plus the famous Black Barn Saturday market in Havelock North during the summer months.

Will the weekend be long enough? What a delicious dilemma!

There's plenty to eat and drink on the Hawke's Bay food trail.

Beer hops and brewery crawls

New Zealand's boutique breweries (including the smaller ones known as micro-breweries) produce more than 250 different beers aimed at the discerning drinker. Checking out some of them can make for a very pleasant weekend.

However, don't overlook a visit to some of the mainstream breweries — Speight's in Dunedin, for example, or Monteith's over on the West Coast, both of which were privately owned for many years but are now in the hands of the brewing giants. They both turn on a fine tour that includes a historic overview and associated memorabilia plus, of course, the opportunity to sample the goods.

In the top half of the North Island there are the likes of DB and Lion as well as specialist operations such as the microbrewery at the Leigh Sawmill Café, where you can enjoy tasting what's on offer or buy some to take home. Up in Whangarei there's the Brauhaus Frings and in the Auckland region you can try a cleansing ale — or whatever takes your fancy — at Galbraith's Alehouse, Hallertau Brewbar, or Waiheke Island Brewery.

Further south the breweries with visitor facilities include Brewers Bar in Mount Maunganui and Waipa Brewery in Rotorua, while over on the east coast Roosters Brew House in Hastings is well worth a detour and for an organic drop you can call in to White Cliffs Brewing Co in Taranaki. DB's Tui brewery, at Mangatainoka, attracts quite a few visitors and once you've made it to the capital, Macs at Shed 22 offers a warm welcome.

In Blenheim the Moa Brewing Company would love to sell you some beer and from there it's not far to Nelson where you'll soon find Founders Organic Brewery, Tasman Brewery (previously Harrington's Brewery), McCashins Brewery & Malthouse, Nelson Bays Brewery and up the road a bit Onekaka's Mussel Inn. A quick trip over to Monteith's on the West Coast could also be in order at this point.

Canterbury boasts the Dux De Lux, Southern Grain Spirits, and the Twisted Hop as well as the big boys, DB and Lion. Finally, way down south (via Speight's in Dunedin) there's the Invercargill Brewery.

By the way, did you realise how long microbrewers have been around in New Zealand? Back in the days of the gold rush, there were small-scale brewers all over the place, including dozens serving the West Coast goldfields.

Speight's has been brewing beer on the same spot in Dunedin since 1876 — find out more on a brewery tour.

Premier pinot

There are very good reasons why quality pinot noir costs as much as it does; low yields, the potential to be damaged by frost, plus frequent hand-picking — they all add up. However, most oenophiles (there's that word again) would agree it's worth every cent. Central Otago is particularly famous for pinot noir, even though it's only been growing here in any significant quantity since the late 1980s — so why not grab your thermals if it's winter (and a lot less if it's summer) and enjoy a weekend in this iconic wine region?

The first fact to grasp is that the region actually comprises six subregions, each with slightly different conditions that combine to produce a fantastic range of wines. There are the cooler areas, such as Gibbston and Wanaka; the warmer ones, such as Bendigo and Bannockburn; Alexandra, which gets very hot indeed; and Lowburn, which boasts the biggest vineyard area of them all. Make sure you leave plenty of time to visit at least a couple of wineries in each subregion — the perfect shortlist could well look something like this: Gibbston Valley Winery, Chard Farm, Rippon Wines, Quartz Reef Bendigo Estate Vineyard, Mt Difficulty Wines, Olssens, Greylands Ridge and Lowburn Ferry Vineyard.

If you're really serious about learning more about this dark and sensual grape, you could align your weekend here with the annual Central Otago Pinot Noir Celebration. This premier wine event, featuring good food and wine along with informed debate on the subject served up with a good dose of fun, attracts several hundred people each year and highlights this special wine variety on a regional, domestic and international basis.

Whether you come here to refine your knowledge about pinot noir or just to enjoy the mind-bogglingly beautiful scenery while you sip, Central Otago will work its magic on you. Salut!

The grapevines turn golden just before harvest at Wooing Tree vineyard.

Beautiful Rippon Vineyard on the shores of Lake Wanaka.

Going organic

Following a food and wine trail is a great way to spend a weekend, but there are times when it's also good to consider your long term health. A couple of days at Levin's Organic River Festival is a thoroughly enjoyable and totally painless way to do this.

Against a background of fantastic and pretty well continuous live music, you can enjoy organic food, wine and beer, attend free workshops on interesting and topical subjects such as sustainability, zero waste and alternative power sources, then go shopping among the health and craft stalls. You can also stock up on natural remedies and find inspiration from a great line-up of motivational speakers. When you're done listening, head for the dance tent and dance your heart out.

This three-day festival, based in Horowhenua, just outside the township of Levin, takes place each summer over Wellington Anniversary Weekend. Back when festival director Malcolm Hadlum first set it up, only about 500 people came, but thousands now turn up each year to enjoy the friendly atmosphere and attractive setting by the river.

It's usually warm and sunny at this time of year so there is plenty of outside — and inside — fun including swimming, fire-pits, drumming, healing, and various forms of massage.

If you want to take the kids with you, they'll be well catered for in the special kids-zone. You could stay in town at any of a number of well priced B&Bs, although many people choose to camp at the festival grounds so they can be right near the action at all times, in which case it's best to book campsites well ahead.

The Organic River Festival is all about creativity and community — so dig out that tent, grab the kids and prepare to have a great weekend.

Plants, crafts and alternative health treatments are on display at Levin's Organic River Festival.

Have an organic beer or wine and soak up some sounds.

Wines and wheels

Why would you want to sit inside a car for the best part of a weekend when you could appreciate the glorious weather and scenic surroundings so much better from a bicycle seat? It's absolutely the best way to enjoy visiting vineyards in the Marlborough region, not least because of the considerately flat countryside, which makes pedalling more enjoyable than challenging.

When you book a cycle tour through this acclaimed wine region, justly famous for its sauvignon blanc and chardonnay varieties, everything you need is provided, starting with courtesy collection and return to wherever you are staying. Then there are the all-important bike and accessories — helmet, bottled water and, crucially, a four-bottle wine pannier. No matter which company you book with, they all offer a full breakdown service and supply detailed maps with which to find your way between the 40-odd wineries within a 10 km radius of Blenheim.

Grapevines stretching towards dry hills — the perfect terrain for cycling.

Visitors to the Allan Scott winery get a taste of Marlborough.

It needn't be all about the wine, however. En route you'll find some very good vineyard cafés and restaurants where you can sit back and enjoy morning coffee, lunch or afternoon tea. Or if you are creatively inclined, ask your tour organiser for directions to the local art and craft galleries. Other goodies available along the way include locally produced olive oil and seasonal fruits, so you could even plan on accumulating enough treats to have a picnic at one of the many scenic spots along the way.

Vineyard cycling tours through this famous region are available all year round. If you plan on taking the kids, just advise the operator at the time of booking and they'll include a child seat or tow-along, as you choose.

Mussels on the menu

The clear, cool waters of the Marlborough Sounds make for great mussels.

New Zealand's green-lipped mussels (trademarked Greenshell) are a vital part of the country's aquaculture, as they are among our most important seafood exports. Now that's a fact worth celebrating — and the mussel festivals held in Marlborough's tiny township of Havelock and the North Island's Coromandel do just that.

In Havelock, aka the 'Greenshell Capital of the World', they've got their Mussel Festival down to a fine art. It's a day that all the family can enjoy, with around 70 stalls showcasing food, wine and beer, crafts and industry displays — there's something for everyone here in this great little community. Mussel opening and mussel munching competitions are among the highlights of the day; they attract heaps of attention from the more than 5000-strong crowd that regularly turns out for the event. All this plus live music from local bands and special guests, together with free entertainment for the kids, adds up to a very good reason for making sure you're in Havelock next March.

Up in Coromandel they've been farming mussels since the early 1980s but the local one-day Mussel Festival is still a fairly

The key to good fritters is to have more mussel than any other ingredient.

new event. However, the enthusiasm both locals and visitors brought to the first one in 2008 will ensure that it becomes a regular family-friendly summer event on the Coromandel calendar.

As with the Havelock event, the purpose behind Coromandel's festival is to celebrate the region's aquaculture industry with great music, markets, competitions and a range of delicious seafood featuring —

you guessed it — mussels cooked every possible way, including the ubiquitous fritters. Wine lovers will be delighted to know the event is licensed so they can match their mussel tasting with a glass of their favourite drop or maybe a cleansing ale, if that is more to their taste.

Live music keeps the crowds buzzing, and a diverse range of stalls featuring arts and crafts and other local products makes for interesting browsing.

Take yourself out to lunch

Eating al fresco — the expression conjures images of a large group of people, usually somewhere in Italy, sitting at a sun-dappled outdoor table that's groaning with loads of good things to eat and drink. As it happens, such a table is not actually that far away. Every summer, eager diners in the know get together in Napier to partake of a fabulous afternoon eating and drinking and enjoying live musical entertainment.

The venue is Napier's Marine Parade gardens and the 250 m long table that's suitably set for the occasion accommodates up to 800 guests (so you'll never be short of interesting dining companions!).

The nationally acclaimed CJ Pask Winery Great Long Lunch takes place in these lovely gardens each year in March. It's the perfect time to be outdoors with the sun overhead and a refreshing, gentle breeze coming off the sea just a few metres away — all this against a backdrop of gorgeous old art deco buildings.

Guests at this unique event are kept in suspense until the last minute regarding the menu, but they can certainly count on being served delicacies from the region's top producers. These are enhanced by award-winning wines from CJ Pask Winery (which is among New Zealand's top merlot producers). In between this relaxing three-course feast, guests are welcome to get some exercise dancing to the great live music. What a fantastic way to justify pigging out on dessert, not to mention the matching wine!

The CJ Pask Winery Great Long Lunch has been going for some years now and its popularity is such that you should book well in advance. So dust off your dancing shoes, or at the very least your best sunhat, and make sure you're one of the happy throng next summer.

Guests enjoy the best of Hawke's Bay wine, food and sunshine.

Up to 800 guests can wine and dine at the
Great Long Lunch.

Wellington Sevens

EVENTS

And they're off!

And they're up and running! If you are anywhere in the vicinity of Christchurch come November, you'd better be sure to have your glad rags to hand. Each year the city celebrates New Zealand Cup and Show Week around this time, but be sure to ask the boss for extra time off because the event actually runs for 10 days.

Cantabrians are justly proud of this fun-filled extravaganza, which has been running since 1996 and which attracts around 125,000 people each year, nearly half of whom are out-of-town visitors. It all came about when Christchurch City Council decided to coordinate the growing number of national-interest races and local events happening in Christchurch over this period, under the New Zealand Cup and Show Week umbrella brand.

Each year the associated trade displays, carnival rides, wine competitions, and food and cooking demonstrations that complement the event vie to be even more appealing to locals and visitors alike. In among all this exciting activity is New Zealand's largest agricultural and pastoral event, the Royal New Zealand Show — three days of indoor and outdoor action-packed family fun.

Great live music is always on offer throughout Cup and Show Week as well as a host of other activities, all planned to fit in with the theme. However, it's horseflesh rather than horse sense that's at the heart of it all, closely followed by an excuse to wear the most extravagant combination of clothes and accessories that you've ever dreamed about. Yes, that's right; Cup and Show Week is also about fashion — and given the number of race meetings that take place during the 10 days, the opportunities for decking yourself out in suitable sartorial style are plentiful indeed. Most importantly, though, are the actual fashion events, including several runway shows featuring national designer collections.

The races themselves, a truly exciting line-up, take part at Addington and Riccarton racecourses and include the New Zealand Galloping and Trotting Cups, Ladies Day, Guineas Day and Show Day.

So go on, cancel that trip to Melbourne, shake out those fancy accessories and get yourself to Christchurch for this unique event.

Horses and hats go together at the New Zealand Cup in Christchurch.

Are you sure that's edible?

In recent years any number of food-related festivals have sprung up and that's a damn good thing whichever way you look at it. But you can't consider yourself a dedicated festival-goer until you've been to the Hokitika Wildfoods Festival, held every year in March. The brainchild of a local woman back in 1990, the very first event attracted around 1800 people. Since then, it's grown considerably and is now quite possibly the premier event on the West Coast. Part of its success must be due to the time of year; over its long proud history the festival has experienced rain on just one occasion.

In addition to offering some rather unusual culinary treats, the festival is all about having a great time, West Coast style. This means, among other things, being treated to some great live music from an assortment of bands and solo artists, while adults are lubricated by the sponsor's product, of course. There's also a chance to win a nice cash prize in the photo competition and accolades for the wildest outfit. Come on, folks — give it a go!

Let's not forget the wild foods. After all, they are what the festival is all about. New wild foods are introduced every year: wasp-larvae ice cream, cucumber fish, sheep's milk cheeses and wok-fried clams are among more recent treats, but you're bound to find some old favourites such as testicle stew, chocolate-dipped huhu grubs and barbecued lambs' tails.

How many different ways can you eat a worm?
Lots, if Hokitika's Wildfoods Festival is any indication.

There are few things they won't eat around here.

The less adventurous may be relieved to hear that a variety of delicious conventional food is also part of the culinary line-up. When the Governor-General attended a recent festival he was heard to say that the classic wild pork and venison were outstanding, as were the whitebait patties he tasted — in fact he claimed they were the best ever!

With this kind of endorsement, you really can't afford to miss out. See you there!

Enjoy a World of Music and Dance

March is a busy month for dedicated festival-goers, who may well find themselves forced to make some difficult decisions about where to go and what to see. Way up the top of your list should be WOMAD, that fabulously funky annual festival celebrating world music, arts and dance. It's spread over three days in Taranaki's New Plymouth.

In recent years as many as 12,000 people have come to watch, listen to or just generally soak up about 60 performances involving 400 artists, divided between multiple stages. Some of these are international legends while others are Kiwi icons, but whatever their status, they all love doing their thing over this action-packed long weekend. All this amazing activity takes

You can expect the unexpected at WOMAD, and not just at ground level.

place in the beautiful setting of Brooklands Park and TSB Bowl, generating a very special atmosphere.

A series of hugely popular artist workshops can provide the opportunity for a once-in-a-lifetime lesson with some of the performing artists and groups; but wait, there's more: outdoor films, on-stage ethnic cooking demonstrations (part of the Taste the World programme) and a 'Global Village' — where more than 80 stalls trade a vast range of international food, beverages and arts and crafts — all make for heaps of family friendly fun. Children are well catered for, too, in a self-contained 'Kidzone' offering five- to twelve-year-olds a structured entertainment and creative programme while under-fives are looked after separately.

A recent WOMAD innovation is the Sustainable Village, which showcases methods, products and companies facilitating sustainable practices. Last but not least, all green-minded attendees will be pleased to know that the clean-up after an event of this magnitude is nothing like other similar-sized festivals, as WOMAD is committed to a 'Zero Waste' strategy (i.e. all waste is recycled in one way or another).

If you can't be there for the whole three days, a bit of planning and early consultation of the schedule, which is released in advance, will ensure you at least get to see your favourite acts.

Full-on world music is just part of the three-day festival experience that Taranaki has claimed as its own.

The big cheese

Who'd have thought that rolling a whole lot of cheese down a hill would become the basis for an annual competition that's now grown into a full-on, fun-filled afternoon in the Deep South? Not only that, but since its inception in 2006 it's also been a highly successful way of raising financial support for Southland and Otago families facing the challenge of autism.

Another gathering designed to make the most of summer, the Whitestone Cheese Rolling takes place in February each year on the Henderson family farm in Wendon Valley, Waikaka, 40 km from Gore. Although it's only been going for a few years, with each successive event it's grown in popularity. It now attracts a good-sized crowd, many of whom have got their eye on the title of New Zealand Champion Cheese Roller — which comes with a cash prize of $500 and a trophy.

The day starts at noon with live music and for the next little while you can either take a helicopter joyride or sample some of the delicious treats available, such as Whitestone cheeses, whitebait fritters, lamb on the spit, and a sausage sizzle. Very special banana splits are also popular and if you've got the kids with you, they'll love getting their faces painted or an energetic session on the giant tiger bouncy castle.

At 2pm the first 4 kg cheese wheel is launched by a celebrity from the top of the hill. Thereafter a cheese wheel takes off every 15 minutes until the Grand Final at 4.30pm. The catcher of each cheese wheel gets to keep it (yum!) so there's a lot of good-natured fun as everyone races down the hill hoping to be one of the lucky ones. Each placegetter takes part in the Grand Final.

Overall, it's a great way to spend part of your weekend in Southland, especially when you consider who benefits at the end.

In Southland, the really big cheese is the person who's best at catching the rolling cheese wheels.

Hop down to the beach

Whether you're young in years or young at heart, if you've a yen to wind back the clock and enjoy life at it was in the 1950s and 60s then the annual Whangamata Beach Hop will be your kind of festival.

This event takes place on the east coast towards the end of each summer. There's a huge variety of entertainment on offer here in the way of music, fashion, hot rods, motorbikes, dancing and much, much more, all of which celebrates this golden era. It's absolutely the place to be if you're keen to impress the crowds with your own Elvis impersonation, collection of 1950s fashion (and matching hairdo!) or your rock'n'roll moves.

Taking place in April, it's a four-day party, a non-stop whirl of excitement punctuated by the roar of hot rods and motorbikes, the likes of which are generally only seen on occasions like this. Other crowd pullers include a drive-in movie, live music, a street festival, talent quests, a beauty competition, a collectable car auction, a classic car show — you name it, if it's anything to do with the 50s and 60s they'll be celebrating it!

The first Beach Hop, a modest one-day affair, was held back in 2001 and raised $3000 for the Onemana and Whangamata surf life-saving clubs and the Whangamata Volunteer Coastguard.

These days upwards of 60,000 people make their way to this popular holiday spot for the hop, with all proceeds donated to emergency services in the area.

Be sure to wear your sunglasses — the sheer dazzle of so much chrome in one place, never mind the hot rods' gloriously colourful paintwork, is enough to give you Technicolor dreams for weeks to come.

Cool cars, hot outfits, beautiful beach — what more could you want!

Non-stop thrills

Every spring thousands of mountain bikers converge on Taupo to take part in what is billed as the largest 12-hour mountain biking event in the world. It all starts in either September or early October in Owen Delany Park on Taupo's Centennial Drive, and be warned — more than 3000 riders are likely to turn up, not to mention all their supporters and a host of spectators.

It's a sporting event with a category for just about everyone: you can compete as an individual or in a team of up to five, and you can choose between the six-hour or twelve-hour event. Both start at 10.30am but the shorter option finishes at 4.30pm while the latter lasts until — yes, you've got it — 10.30pm. No wonder it's called the Day Night Thriller!

While the circuit, the same for both grades, is only 8 km long, it's been specifically designed to cater to riders of all abilities. It covers fast open park terrain, awesome downhill stretches, pine-needle-covered forest tracks, challenging narrow one-way tracks and a whole lot of magnificent scenery — including the majestic Waikato River.

Accommodation in Taupo is rarely a problem because there are just so many places to choose from. However, if you're taking part in the Thriller, or there to support a team, you might want to set up camp along with all the others at Owen Delany Park, where the atmosphere positively buzzes all weekend.

If you've got mountain-biking-proficient kids between the ages of eight and thirteen, why not sign them up for the Hell Pizza Little Devils' Ride? It's an exciting 7 km ride starting at 9.15am. It involves one lap of the Day Night track, through tent city to the finish line, and is fully supervised by experienced mountain-bike riders.

The Taupo day-and-night event offers plenty of thrills — with hopefully not too many spills!

Join more than 3000 riders, or be one of many spectators watching from a safe distance.

Peace and plenty

It's a wonderful thing indeed that a place such as Parihaka, which back in the nineteenth century was the site of one of the worst infringements of civil rights ever committed in this country, has since 2006 been the scene of an annual international peace festival.

For most of the year, Parihaka is a small settlement made up of unassuming buildings and homes. However, early each year (soon after New Year), several thousand people descend on the township, each committed to achieve the festival's goal of 'facing the challenges, being a part of the solutions' as part of a festival community of 'truly open-hearted and open-minded people who are there to share the experience and promote peaceful living'.

As you'd expect, most if not all of the people attending this three-day festival are into zero waste and organic, sustainable lifestyles, and the prevailing activity, including performances and educational presentations, workshops and screenings, is representative of these goals. It's not all serious, however — there's always a great line-up of live acts, including music, food stalls (rumour has it the hangi is positively sublime), and arts and crafts featuring some interesting and creative sculptures.

Be sure to bring camping equipment, along with sunhats and shade for the daytime and warm clothing for the evenings. You'll be pleased to know that as the festival has grown so have the facilities; there are more than enough Portaloos and gas-powered showers on the farmland where camping sites have been established. As for the event's alcohol policy, it's open but relies heavily on people respecting themselves and each other. You'll need to leave glass containers and pets at home and be prepared to take any plastic waste home with you.

Previous Parihaka festivals have had a golf-cart shuttle service to help people — particularly older people and tired parents and children — move around comfortably, making it a very enjoyable event for all ages.

The historic landscape at Parihaka, southwest of New Plymouth, is now host to an annual music festival.

All that jazz

Tauranga vistors and locals alike can enjoy the downtown carnival feeling and al fresco dining.

If an event's longevity plays a part in deciding which weekend music festival to attend, then Tauranga's National Jazz Festival would have to win hands down. It's been going strong for close to 50 years now and the great acts, as well as the numbers attending each year, just keep growing.

Held over Easter, the festival is a great way of soaking up some seriously good jazz as well as enjoying a long weekend in the Bay of Plenty; but given its popularity you do need to book ahead — recent years have seen people coming from as far afield as the United States.

The festival features a number of musical acts spread over a variety of venues — including a concert series boasting big names both on the local and international scene, and a jazz club where you can pre-order food platters to nibble at while you take in the music. There's also a dedicated jazz village with several stages; these include an outdoor one and one for jam sessions that see plenty of live action. Complementing all this activity are assorted buskers, barbershop quartets and, of course, food stalls offering a range of hot and cold treats to help you keep your strength up. There's plenty on offer for the kids in the jazz village, too — for example, at Huckleberry Finn's Music Den they can be as creatively noisy as they like in the drumming and 'blow your trumpet' workshops.

It's possible to spend much of the festival just cruising and listening to live music.

Recent novelty events that may become a regular part of the festival involved a cruise around the harbour on a riverboat and a two-hour trip on a classic steam train, both of which featured live jazz bands.

Another popular part of the festival is the Downtown Tauranga Carnival that runs over two afternoons in the middle of the city. There's no charge to listen to the live music and you can have a very enjoyable time moving from one stage to another, with perhaps a refreshment stop or two at any of the city's bars and restaurants along the way.

Pay homage to Burt

New Zealanders have an endearing habit of taking underdogs to their hearts. A shining example of this attitude is the Burt Munro Challenge, proudly presented by the Southland Motorcycle Club as 'one hell of a weekend' that's enjoyed each year by thousands of motorcycling enthusiasts. For the record, Burt Munro was the bloke who claimed the World Record Class S-A 1000 cc on his modified Indian Scout motorbike with an average speed of 183.586 mph back in 1967 — a record that stands to this day.

Throughout the three-day event, which traditionally takes place in the last weekend of November each year, bike aficionados can have a wonderful time inhaling the fumes as they watch various races including speedway, track and street racing, then dance up a storm at night in the specially constructed marquee.

One of the highlights of the weekend is when the Competitor of the Year Burt Munro Family Trophy, a memorial to Burt Munro's 'originality, ingenuity, creativity, tenacity and determination to overcome obstacles in both engineering and riding', is awarded.

Another highlight is the beach racing. Oreti Beach, 10 km out of Invercargill, was a key location for the film *The World's Fastest Indian*. It was here that Burt Munro set a New Zealand Open Beach record of 131.38 mph in early 1957, and where in 1975 he raised it to 136 mph.

Where you stay is up to you but it's worth knowing that you can camp free of charge at Oreti Park. What's more, there are loads of food stalls so you don't even have to bring supplies with you. There's even a cooked breakfast on Saturday and Sunday morning for a very reasonable fee, provided you preorder it when you register.

After all the excitement is over and before you head back to your own neck of the woods, go and have a gander at Munro's original Indian, which is on display at E Hayes & Sons, the city's longest-established hardware and engineering shop.

Wannabe Burt Munros get on their bikes during the annual Burt Munro Challenge.

A festival of wine

Can you imagine a nicer way to spend a summer weekend than at a festival celebrating wine in one of New Zealand's most scenic locations? Each February, for quite a few years now the town of Blenheim has been proudly hosting the annual Marlborough Wine Festival, a major event on the country's wine calendar.

Some people get a head start and arrive a day or two before the official fun starts, but for those with more limited time, the festival kicks off on the Friday with the annual Festival Market Day. It's advisable to equip yourself with a large shopping bag because you'll want to take home lots of goodies from the array of arts, crafts, food and clothing on offer. You'd also be wise to book your choice of restaurant for that night well ahead, because by late afternoon the town will be heaving with visitors.

The actual festival takes place on the Saturday out at Brancott Estate, starting at 10.30am and going through until 6pm. Shuttle buses run between the town and the festival venue all day, and there's no need to bring a picnic because everything you could possibly want in the way of gourmet foods is here.

Around 40 local wineries showcase their range of wines, which means there are about 200 different labels to choose from. As you wander around sipping and tasting, you'll be entertained by a fabulous line-up of live music and you can even sign up for a wine tutorial or two.

The third day of this full-on festival comes with a couple of choices: a day out on the water or a tour around the region's cellar doors. If you choose the former, you'll be transported to Havelock where you'll board a launch for a cruise out to Kenepuru Sound, which includes a couple of glasses of bubbly and a two-course lunch. However, if you go for the cellar-door bus tour, lunch is an optional extra — and although you won't know where you'll be having it until you get there, you can be sure it'll be a good one given the reputation of the region's fantastically fresh and tasty produce.

Note that Marlborough is famous for the number of sunshine hours so make sure you've got your full complement of slip, slap, slop gear with you.

Become a wine connoisseur at the Marlborough Wine Festival.

Marlborough's Brancott Estate plays host on the Saturday of the festival.

   E V E N T S

Chocolate-coated fun

July tends to be a quieter time of year in terms of the number of festivals taking place around the country, which is just as well, because when it comes to eating chocolate you don't want anything else getting in the way.

The Cadbury Chocolate Carnival, sponsored and run by both the Dunedin City Council and Cadbury, has been a highlight on Dunedin's winter calendar since 2002 and now comprises seven days of sweet events, some of which are free and many of which are low cost. Not everyone is able to get away for a whole week, of course, and if you find yourself in this unenviable position you'll have the agonising task of deciding what you can and can't miss out on. For example, it'd be a great shame not to be present at the famous Jaffa Roll. This event involves rolling giant Jaffas (round balls of orange-candy-coated chocolate confectionery) down Baldwin Street, which is claimed to be the world's steepest street — all in the name of fundraising (one of the carnival's main aims is to raise money for selected charities) — with up to 30,000 Jaffas, each individually numbered, making the ultimate sacrifice. Then there are the cooking demonstrations, chocolate art classes, chocolate therapy and chocolate facials. Let's face it — you really need to be here for the whole week.

Another must-see is the Chocolate Fair in the Octagon. If you've got the kids in tow, then the Cadbury Kids' Bake-off has to be part of your programme. Other child-friendly events include the Gnaughty Gnomes and Fabulous Fairies party at Glenfalloch, a teddy bears' picnic at Larnach Castle and chocolate fishing on the MV *Monarch*. After your little ones have enjoyed such great entertainment, consider rewarding yourself with a night of chocolate, jazz and shiraz, an event that's strictly for grown-ups.

Street entertainment is just one of the attractions of the Cadbury Chocolate Carnival.

Be ready to indulge in all
sorts of ways.

Island of olives

It's been estimated that there are now something like 1.5 million olive trees flourishing in our countryside. It's an impressive number and one that's worth celebrating; something Waiheke Island's Everything Olive Festival does in grand style every November at the Rangihoua Estate olive grove.

Running over two days, the festival is a very enjoyable and laid-back affair at which you can fully indulge your taste for olive oil.

Aficionados will already know that the island is home to several award-winning oil producers, which makes the festival the perfect opportunity to meet some of them and learn about the trials and tribulations of growing and harvesting this ancient crop. It's also a chance to test your tastebuds on some of the different varieties available — and impress your friends by talking convincingly about the desirability of peppery notes or flavours such as grass cuttings. If you're not as familiar with the features and benefits of locally produced extra-virgin olive oil as you'd like to be, then the free seminars each day will be just the thing. You'll also get to inspect the Rangihoua olive press room.

Meanwhile, musicians will be doing their thing out in the grove. You might want to bring a picnic to enjoy while you listen to the live music, but it's more likely you'll want to sample some of the goodies on offer such as oysters, paella and pizza —

all washed down naturally enough with a glass or two of Waiheke Island wines.

Once you've had enough good food and sun, head back indoors to the olive tasting room and treat yourself to a bottle or three of extra-virgin oil to take home. With all those salads and barbecues planned for the summer months, you won't regret it!

Waiheke's olives are celebrated and much good music, food and wine are enjoyed at the island's annual olive festival.

Victorian splendour

The South Island city of Oamaru is a handsome place, bristling with nineteenth-century architecture that in November each year is enhanced by the presence of hundreds of people dressed to match in Victorian costumes.

The highlight of Oamaru's heritage weekend is a grand Victorian ball, but on either side of that are lots of different activities including a Grand Victorian Street Parade where — as you'd expect — nearly everyone dons period costume. There are also vintage cars, traction engines and tractors, and a vintage fire truck (which came in handy one year when a vintage tractor caught fire).

A fête is also part of the annual line-up. In recent years this has included as many as 100 stalls (offering everything from German bratwurst to unicorns, clothes for teddy bears and palm readings) lining the roadside. Once again, all participants are resplendent in Victorian-style dress.

Another highlight is the beard and moustache competition whose prize is awarded to the wildest, woolliest set of whiskers. The Oamaru stone-sawing championships, national penny-farthing races, Highland pipe and garrison bands, tribal drummers, horses, Morris dancers and jugglers, as well as a Servants and Swaggers Dance, are all part of the fun, too. And let's not forget the annual trolley derby down Tyne Street — thrills and spills being the order of the day at this particular event.

When you visit Oamaru for its heritage weekend, don't worry if you don't have your own suitably Victorian ensemble; just make sure you contact the Victorian Wardrobe, a project run by the Oamaru Whitestone Civic Trust, which hires out possibly the largest and finest collection of Victorian-styled clothes anywhere in New Zealand. It's a great opportunity to indulge your passion for dressing up and all for a good cause, too — the proceeds from the weekend are used to help the Oamaru Whitestone Civic Trust preserve the Harbour and Tyne Historic Precinct.

Penny-farthings take to the streets for the annual Oamaru heritage festival.

Oamaru is blessed with a precinct of
grand old Victorian buildings.

Rockin' the bay

OK, all you country rockers — dust off your Stetsons, iron your shirts, polish your boots, and head to the Far North. For one long weekend each May the normally tourist-focused town of Paihia turns its attention to other equally important matters, such as country music and line dancing.

Back in its early days the festival focused almost entirely on country and western music, and while over the years it has evolved into a popular community event, appealing to all ages and tastes, it still ranks as one of the premier country music events in Australasia.

Local acts include the likes of Marian Burns, the Heartleys, and Cactus Jack, while Australian musicians such as Craig Byrne, Dennis Morgan, Patrick Robertson, Stephen R Cheney, David and Merelyn Carter and Laura Downing also feature. Then there are the big names that come all the way from Nashville, Tennessee. Obviously these vary from year to year, but the one constant is the effort put in by the organisers to ensure everyone has a good time.

Line dancing is a major part of the festival, with participants known as 'boot scooters'. Each year the dancing starts on Friday night, going through until Sunday night with only minimal breaks for sleep and refreshments.

In recent years the festival programme has featured a 'walk up' segment, in which anyone who's busting to prove their blood is pumping with country and western corpuscles can get up and have a go. The ferry people are in on the action, too; over the years a music cruise has been a very popular part of the festival.

All up, the annual Bay of Islands Country Rock Festival boasts 200 hours of country music, which has to be enough to satisfy even the most committed fans of the genre.

Line dancers put their best foot forward in Paihia.

You'll have a boot-scootin' good time at the Bay of Islands Country Rock Festival.

Score at the Sevens

Since 1999 thousands upon thousands of people have flocked to the country's capital city each February, all eager to be infected by rugby sevens fever. It's one of the most contagious conditions you can suffer from in the sporting world — although this colourful tournament's main focus is not necessarily sport.

Sixteen international teams compete for points that go towards the International Rugby Board Sevens World Series, but it's what goes on before, during and after the games that turns Wellington into what has been called a slightly paler version of Rio de Janeiro's Mardi Gras carnival.

Tickets sold out within 10 minutes for a recent tournament, which is pretty impressive when you consider that Wellington's Westpac Stadium on Waterloo Quay, where the games are played, holds around 34,500 people.

If you don't know what the Wellington Sevens is all about and want to experience it for yourself, there are just a few things you should know. First and foremost, get your tickets in plenty of time. Then you'll need to start planning the most outrageous costume you can think of and be prepared to wear it for the full two days of the event. But be warned — there'll be some pretty stiff competition! Many regular attendees come along for this amazing tournament's social aspects, which are a big part of it all (as well as a good excuse to let go of all your inhibitions). However, be aware there are limits — even at a Sevens tournament. Wearing a Borat-style swimsuit, for example, is frowned upon by the police (and who can blame them!), as is taking alcohol into the stadium.

Otherwise, just go with the flow and let yourself enjoy every minute of this distinctly un-Wellington two-day costumed extravaganza.

Rugby? What rugby? The crowd gets into the party mood at the Wellington Sevens.

During the Sevens weekend it's a point of honour to match your mates — whatever they come up with.

101 MUST-DO WEEKENDS · AA

Opunake, Taranaki

ROAD
TRIPS

Surfin' Highway 45

Taranaki has a reputation for some of the best surfing beaches in New Zealand so it's not surprising that the dream of most New Zealand surfers, old and young, is to take some time out to explore Surf Highway 45.

Beginning in Hawera, the 100 km route follows the highly scenic Taranaki coastline through many of the country's best surfing spots (it features some excellent windsurfing spots, too). Because it's not an enormous distance, you can spend as much or as little time on the trip as you have available. But it would be a shame to rush if you don't have to . . .

For the experienced surfer the following descriptions of some of the major surf breaks en route will make perfect sense. However, if you're a beginner you may find hanging around the clubs in the region will help you become familiar with the lingo. Another option is to take surfing lessons, and down this coast you'll find plenty of teachers.

Starting in south Taranaki and working your way north, check out these surf breaks: Ohawe Beach (right hander, fast, popular for swimming and fishing); Mangahume (A-frame, challenging waves in northeasterly wind); the Dump (best at lower tide); Opunake Beach (right hander, high tide, offshore northeasterly wind); Arawhata Road (right break; left and right in middle of bay); Kina Road (popular windsurfing spot); Stent Road (five spots, working on all tides, offshore northeasterly); Graveyards (left hander, southeasterly wind); Rocky Point: Rocky Rights (northeasterly wind) and Rocky Lefts (southeasterly wind); Weld Road (good longboard spot); Ahu Ahu Road (gentle left hander and fast right hander); Oakura Beach (local club spot, beach break); Back Beach (west facing, bars change frequently, deceptive wave size); East End Beach (northwest facing, best at mid high tide); Fitzroy Beach (local club spot, barrels, right and left hander); and Waiwhakaiho River Mouth and Groyne (left and right off A-frame peak).

> **Surf life-savers are available at Oakura, south of New Plymouth, to lend a hand.**

A surfer shoots the barrel in some gnarly Taranaki surf.

Riding a thermal

When you've got a tankful of gas, a back seat full of kids and a weekend full of free time, that's an excellent time to explore the Thermal Explorer Highway. If you're wanting to drive the whole route from go to whoa, it helps if you're at either the Auckland end or the Napier end, although there's no reason why you couldn't join the route along the way.

Starting a little south of Auckland, this road trip takes in much of the Waikato, passing the sacred Maori burial ground of Taupiri Mountain, and Turangawaewae Marae, home of the Maori King, just off the main road. The mighty Waikato River swirls past for a good part of this segment of the trip and it's awfully tempting to stop and have a picnic on its banks.

Once you've had your fill of the Waikato

The steaming Cathedral Rock is just one of the attractions at Waimangu Thermal Valley.

Nowhere does boiling mud like Rotorua.

and its fertile plains, round up the kids and point the car towards either Rotorua or Waitomo. If you go for the former, you'll have some serious soaking in a hot pool to look forward to, not to mention a host of wonderful tourist sights to take in including bubbling mud pools, steaming geysers, and Maori cultural events — you certainly won't be disappointed. Nor will you be if you choose to drop in on the glow-worms at Waitomo Caves (and you can always call in at Rotorua on the way back!). Next stop is the central volcanic plateau where, if the sky is clear, you can admire the magnificent peaks of Ruapehu, Tongariro and Ngauruhoe in the distance. If you've got a keen angler

in the car, why not stop and let them try their luck at catching a trout?

Don't forget to stop at Huka Falls just outside Taupo; the sheer power of the water as it shoots over the rocky drop has to be seen to be believed!

Back in the car, head east over the Ahimanawa Range, but be sure to top up the fuel tank because between Taupo and Hawke's Bay there are no petrol stations.

A few hours later and you're in the heart of the Hawke's Bay region, with its huge range of gourmet treats, fresh produce and award-winning wine. So go on — make the most of it before it's time to turn around and go home. Sigh . . .

The Huka Falls, near Taupo, make for spectacular photographs.

Get lost in a forgotten world

It's really quite amazing that in such a small country as ours we have so many alternative routes criss-crossing between the smaller centres. One excellent example is the 150 km Forgotten World Highway that connects the North Island towns of Stratford and Taumarunui. This region has so much going for it that a weekend spent down here is well worth the effort involved (for example, Taranaki Mount Egmont, wild coastlines and bush walks, not to mention small-town hospitality . . .).

Whichever starting point you choose — Stratford or Taumarunui — make sure you fill the fuel tank before you head off, because you could be waiting a long time for a good samaritan to pass by with a container of petrol in their boot.

The Forgotten World Highway was established in 1990 to provide travellers on State Highway 43 with an opportunity to experience first hand the history of the bush-clad hills comprising the route. As you drive you'll spot the vestiges of

It's gorgeous, it's remote, and there's no petrol for several hundred kilometres.

Once the heart of a farm, this shed stands sentinel near Tangarakau on the Lost Highway.

homes people tried to build here many years ago, but the environment in the end proved just too tough . . .

As you make your way along this route take time to appreciate the scenery: from the top of the ragged Strathmore Saddle the three volcanoes of Tongariro National Park are visible to the east along with the snow-topped cone of Taranaki Mount Egmont to the west; from the Whangamomona Saddle there are magnificent views of native beech and podocarp forest (there's also a great three-hour circular walk that begins here); and from Tahora Saddle not only can you see the central plateau volcanoes, but also several historic pa sites on hilltops to the west and east. A bit of a detour down the Moki Forest Road to Mount Damper Falls will reward you with the sight of one of the highest waterfalls in the North Island.

If you think you might need a refreshment stop along the way, we suggest you take a picnic, or save yourself until you reach the historic hotel in Whangamomona.

The wild, wild west

Prepare for a unique experience if you are planning a driving weekend on the West Coast of the South Island — it's a winner any way you look at it, in terms of historical interest, scenery and hospitality.

Depending on which way you have arrived on the coast (via the Buller George or Lewis Pass in the north, Arthur's Pass in the centre or the Haast Pass in the south), there is a wealth of things to see.

The remains of the once-busy coal-mining town at Denniston are fascinating to explore.

Starting from the town of Westport in the Buller District, you might visit the Coaltown Museum, or drive up the winding road to the ruins of the coalmining town of Denniston, spectacularly sited at the top of a precipitous railway incline.

If thinking about coalmining makes you feel hot and dusty, head back to the West Coast Brewery for a refreshing ale. Depending on the time of year, you might want to check out the beach, but if the water is too cold you can go and watch the fur seals at nearby Cape Foulwind.

When it's time to get back in the car, head south on State Highway 6 to Punakaiki, home of the famous Pancake Rocks and blowholes — they really are worth visiting and are only a 20-minute loop walk from the carpark near the main highway.

Keep heading south on State Highway 6 down to Greymouth, the largest town on the coast. Be prepared to drink more beer, because a must-do while in Greymouth is a visit to the original Monteith's Brewery.

South of Greymouth there's more heritage and natural splendour on the cards: the re-created goldrush Shantytown, the real-life gold town of Ross, then check out the jade carvers of Hokitika. Further south again, if you can extend your weekend, are the awe-inspiring Fox and Franz Josef glaciers.

Franz Josef Glacier pokes its snout out of the mountains.

The far east

When you feel like getting away from it all, a long slow trip around the East Cape of the North Island is a great way to replenish your spirits. It offers a combination of splendid isolation, magnificent coastal scenery, interesting driving conditions, hot springs and much more besides.

Most people would agree that the journey starts somewhere between Whakatane and Opotiki, a fairly loose but pleasant starting point — especially during summer when most people would kill to be anywhere near the beaches here.

The road is State Highway 35, also known as the Pacific Highway, a name that conjures up all sorts of seaside images — and rest assured, the reality won't let you down. It's a particularly well signposted route along which it's perfectly possible to reach Gisborne within six hours. But why would you want to rush? Ahead of you lies mile after mile of pristine coastline, interspersed with small townships where you can stop for some local hospitality and perhaps investigate some of the historic buildings you'll find.

There are also countless examples of Eastland entrepreneurship such as little galleries and studios showcasing local artisan talent. Other must-do activities include a soak in the hot springs at Morere; a visit to Whangara, where the acclaimed movie *Whale Rider* was filmed; and a walk along the historic wharf at Tolaga Bay,

around 50 km north of Gisborne. Built in the 1920s, this is the longest wharf in the country and there's a lot of effort currently going into restoring it. While you're in this area, stretch your legs on Cook's Cove Walkway (at the southern end of Tolaga Bay) to see the place where the great captain stopped to stock up on supplies and repair his ship back in 1769.

And finally, plan on staying a night in Gisborne at the end of your road trip (or the beginning if you are heading north), so you can be among the first people in the world to see the sun the next morning.

The East Cape road trip offers golden weather and Kiwi heritage to explore.

Several historic communities lie along
State Highway 35, begging to be explored.

Triangle of delights

Wherever you are in the South Island, you're never far from some fantastic scenery and a bunch of exciting outdoor activities. This is especially true of the area defined by the Alpine Pacific Triangle touring route, which takes in Hanmer Springs, the Waipara Valley wine region and the seaside town and whale-watching mecca of Kaikoura.

These days, people come from all over the place to see and learn about the whales that regularly visit this part of the coastline. Not much more than a hundred years ago, however, it was a different story, when the beaches of Kaikoura witnessed the slaughter of huge numbers of these magnificent mammals.

There are also plenty of other examples of marine life to see (including dolphins, seals, penguins and a variety of seabirds), as well as Fyffe House, the town's oldest surviving building and a beautifully preserved slice of history.

Once you've had your fill of this ruggedly picturesque part of the coast, head inland to Hanmer Springs. Everyone knows about its soothing thermal pools, but there's also lots of other stuff to do here. There's fishing, tramping, quad biking, golf, horse riding . . . or maybe you'd rather indulge yourself in some of the delicious range of treats on offer at one of the town's many cafés. Go on, then . . . you know you want to!

Not far away, in the tiny little town of Waiau, the Cob Cottage Museum is well worth visiting to learn how people used to live in this area, through a fascinating collection of domestic and other memorabilia.

Finish the trip at Waipara, where local winemakers have turned the region into an oenophile's paradise — you'll certainly be spoilt for choice!

The Alpine Pacific Triangle's touring route offers plenty to the outdoor enthusiast.

FRESH COOKED CRAYFISH

NIN'S BIN

LOBSTER OPEN

BOAT SAFETY CHECK LIST
Before you go, check:-
WEATHER
LIFE JACKETS
OARS / FUEL
BAILER   ANCHOR
DISTRESS SIGNALS
EXTINGUISHERS
And tell someone
where you're going!

Kaikoura equals seafood. Stopping for a feed of cray is all part of the journey.

Sand, surf and spirits

While most Kiwis would agree that all of our country is special, some bits deserve to be singled out over others. One of these is at the top of the North Island, where a slender finger of land spreads out at the very tip, with Cape Reinga presiding on the western side.

This is where State Highway 1 finishes, and the point at which anyone wanting to travel further needs to get hold of some kind of amphibious craft.

All jokes aside, Cape Reinga is a very special place to visit, not least because of its place in Maori lore (it's from here that souls are said to leap into the ocean to strike out for the spiritual homeland of Hawaiki). As you stand here, it's actually possible to see the waves of the Tasman Sea clash against those of the Pacific Ocean — is there anywhere else in the world where you can witness such an amazing sight?

The drive up there is a wonderful road trip in itself. However, it's absolutely essential you go off road for at least part of the trip to experience driving along Nainety Mile Beach (which is in reality a mere 60 odd miles, or about 100 km, but let's not allow the facts to get in the way of a good story). For obvious reasons, you'll need to check out the tide times; the beach is most vehicle friendly three hours either side of high tide. When you're within cooee of the giant sand dunes, park the car somewhere safe and indulge your inner child in a wild ride down the steep surface of the dunes. This will definitely get your appetite going, so on the way back the budget conscious can stop for fish'n'chips at Whatawhiwhi on the Karikari Peninsula, or, if the money's flowing, at Carrington Resort, a luxury lodge with its own vineyard and a fabulous golf course.

If it's summertime, consider pre-booking one of DOC's fabulous campsites (see page 38) in the region and spend a night or two up here.

Unless you're a bird, Cape Reinga is the end of the road for most travellers.

Untouched sand dunes back Ninety Mile Beach.

Waikoropupu Springs, Golden Bay

HIDDEN
TREASURES

The world comes to Manawatu

Not much in life is free these days, but the good old city council in Palmerston North have made it their business to sponsor an annual Festival of Cultures in March of each year — to acknowledge and celebrate the art, culture and lifestyle of the Manawatu region's many cultural communities.

The event, which encompasses around 30 different cultures, always draws a good-sized crowd; in recent years at least 10,000 people have joined in the fun that kicks off at 10am one Saturday in March with a world food, craft and music fair in the city's square. All-day entertainment and traditional cultural foods and crafts, art and music make it a great day for everyone, particularly families. Be sure to bring an appetite so you can properly enjoy the tantalising aromas and delicious tastes of different cultures' cuisine from the many food stalls. You can also enjoy the sights and sounds of top-quality live entertainment from representatives of every continent. Stick around until the end of the day: shortly after 5pm a colourful grand parade around the square concludes the fair before the start of the evening's entertainment programme, which is usually an outdoor concert featuring local acts and international entertainers.

Over the next few days, the community gets to enjoy live theatre, music, various events at the main library, and a Cultural Schools Education Programme. Local cafés and bars are all part of the action, too, with the festival organisers ensuring they host cultural music wherever possible.

Sporting fans are not forgotten, either: a soccer tournament suitably named Ethkick has been set up to promote a positive image of social cohesion and friendship through sport. With around 100 different ethnic groups within the Manawatu there's usually no shortage of team members.

Bejewelled and painted, a young performer knows she's got what it takes to get noticed.

The festival features around 30 different cultures and their music, dance and food.

Chinese dragon dancers on stage at the Manawatu Festival of Cultures.

A secret in Central

With Ranfurly at its centre, the area known as the Maniototo can be found by following State Highway 85 from Palmerston or approaching from Queenstown via Alexandra or from Dunedin. Comprising a sprawling plain nourished by the Taieri River, the Maniototo is home to a small but fervently loyal population distributed among a number of small towns. People who live here are fiercely jealous of their territory and woe betide anyone who speaks or acts less than respectfully of its charms, which as it happens are legion. Even the air looks and tastes different to that of the rest of Central Otago so it's hardly surprising the locals feel so strongly about their special place.

There are no prizes for guessing the nationality of surveyor JT Thompson who, back in the 1850s, was responsible for the range of colourful names that stud the region: names such as Eweburn, Sowburn, Wedderburn, Gimmerburn, Pigburn, Kyeburn, Hogburn clearly indicate that he could only have come from a farming background in Scotland.

However, it wasn't until the heady days of the gold rush that the Maniototo came to the attention of the rest of the world. In the 1860s thousands of miners eager to stake a claim descended on the area and before long a number of towns catering to their every need sprang up. Over time some of these sank quietly back into the ground, leaving little trace, while others took on a

The Maniototo is scattered with reminders of past habitants.

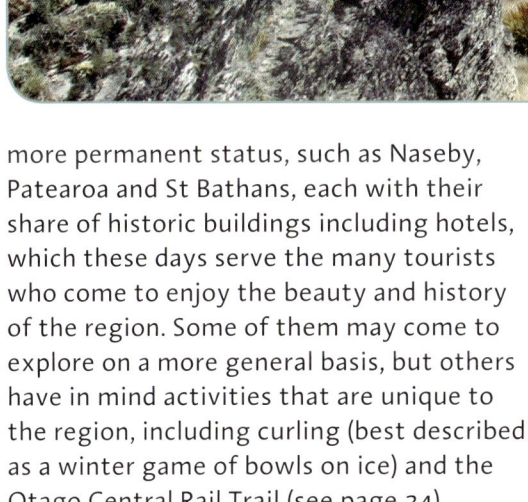

more permanent status, such as Naseby, Patearoa and St Bathans, each with their share of historic buildings including hotels, which these days serve the many tourists who come to enjoy the beauty and history of the region. Some of them may come to explore on a more general basis, but others have in mind activities that are unique to the region, including curling (best described as a winter game of bowls on ice) and the Otago Central Rail Trail (see page 34).

Whatever your reason for coming here, take time to appreciate a pace of life that most of us are not lucky enough to experience in our everyday lives.

Curling is a popular sport, either on frozen dams or indoors.

Gardens of paradise

The annual Taranaki Rhododendron and Garden Festival, which has been going strong since the late 1980s, offers all those with green thumbs (along with those who aspire to such a condition) the chance to see a stunning range of gardens and events. Taking place in late October each year, the festival is the perfect excuse to make your way to Taranaki and enjoy a fun weekend driving yourself around the region's very special gardens.

Close to 50 of them open their gates during this popular event, including a number of gardens of national and regional significance. Each of these is judged against a list of very strict criteria so you know you are only seeing the very best. In fact, this festival features the highest concentration of such high-quality gardens anywhere in the country, with several ranking alongside some of the great gardens of the world.

It's not possible to list every garden open to visitors during the festival but it pays to know they are spread right around the Taranaki region, providing the opportunity to inspect — and be inspired by — a wide range of landscaping and imaginative uses of exotic and indigenous plants, from alpine to forest varieties.

Many of them are private gardens showcasing the talents of skilled domestic landscapers, and are open only while the festival is on. However, others are open all year round, including Pukeiti, New Zealand's

Woodleigh Gardens near Oakura features one of New Zealand's finest collections of hydrangeas.

premier rhododendron garden, which is set in lush rainforest and whose 12 specific garden areas showcase different collections or groupings of plants. Pukekura Park is another great garden destination where it would be all too easy to spend the best part of a day enjoying the magnificent trees, lawns, lakes and streams interlinked by tranquil shady footpaths (equipping yourself with a picnic lunch would be a fine idea here).

During the festival, you can pick up a map that shows all the relevant gardens in the region.

Pukeiti is the country's premier rhododendron garden.

Taranaki is in bloom during the annual Rhododendron and Garden Festival.

Over the 10 days of the festival, an interesting range of workshops, guest speakers and garden-related events runs concurrently. But be warned — you'll need more than a weekend to visit every single garden.

A walk on the Waihi side

As we all know, it takes a bunch of motivated people to get things done. And they're definitely not short of motivation in the Bay of Plenty town of Waihi, which must be why they have such a splendid network of walking tracks that make this corner of the country a great place to spend a weekend.

You can choose between a gentle stroll or a more energetic experience — or perhaps both depending on how much time and energy you have to spend. Given you're likely to be staying in or around the town, however, why not start off with an investigation of the Martha goldmine's Pit Rim Walkway? You'll learn lots about the mine's workings and be rewarded at the end with a breathtaking view from the lookout at the top of the pit's north wall.

A walk upstream along the replanted banks of the Ohinemuri River and then up a track to the summit of Black Hill makes for another pleasant outing. Once again, a fabulous view awaits. When you're ready to head out of town, the Orokawa and Homunga Walkway will lead you from the northern end of Waihi Beach to beautiful, secluded Orokawa Bay, taking in spectacular views of the Pacific Ocean and Waihi Beach. It takes about half an hour, and once you're there you can extend your walk by following the marker posts along a slightly tougher 1.5 km bush track to the 28 m high William Wright Falls.

Waihi Beach, viewed from the Orokawa Walkway.

It's also worth exploring the Karangahake Gorge via the Windows Walk (see page 16), with its old mining tunnels, ore-roasting kilns and tramways. From the Karangahake Reserve, put your best foot forward on a swing bridge across the river. Once on the other side, take some time to absorb the spectacular scenery as well as a fascinating array of goldrush remnants.

Another excellent trip takes you up through Scotsmans Gully onto Karangahake mountain, where the No. 7 level track offers amazing views into the gorge. Follow the Dubbo 96 Track down to Dickey Flat, and from there follow the Waitewheta River back to the reserve. A five-hour round trip will take walkers to the top of the mountain for panoramic views over the surrounding countryside.

Take a dip at Owharoa Falls in the
Karangahake Gorge, near Waihi.

Blooming wonderful

The longest-running community event of its kind in New Zealand, the annual Blossom Festival held in the small town of Alexandra in Central Otago is, unsurprisingly, a spring event held in September each year. Thanks to the wide range of related activities on offer, you could actually extend your weekend to two weeks in this part of the world and still not see everything associated with the event. From woolshearing competitions, fashion parades, dances, and arts and crafts workshops and stalls, to amusement rides, garden tours and cycling rides — this golden oldie of a festival has something for everyone.

The festival kicks off with a competition to race up and around the Alexandra clock tower. However, this race is not about relying on your legs to get you there — competitors use a variety of props that inevitably provide some great entertainment.

Naturally enough, the main focus of the festival is on the blossoms themselves, which proliferate each spring on the multitude of local fruit trees (Alexandra is famous for its stone fruits). Thus the street procession that takes place on the first Saturday of the festival is, as you'd expect after 50-odd years, a magnificent affair, with float after gloriously colourful float each created out of thousands of blossoms.

Of course you can't have a parade of

this nature without a couple of winners: best street procession float and, of course, Blossom Princess are the two most hotly contested titles. Voting for these takes place in the park, with the awards ceremony a part of Saturday in the Park, a family-friendly extravaganza attracting thousands of visitors. Live music, food stalls, entertainment for the kids plus some great arts and crafts all make this a very enjoyable part of the festival.

The garden tour is another must-see component of the festival and features a wide range of attractive gardens that differ in size and style. Definitely enough to inspire even the most jaded gardener.

It all adds up to an extravaganza of colour that you really have to attend at least once.

Spring has sprung and Alexandra is all dressed up and ready to party.

Golden days in the bay

Find out if these beauties know the difference between a finger and eel food at Bencarri.

Tucked away in the South Island's northwest corner is a relatively small but very special region — one that tends to be overlooked by many because it's not actually on the way to anywhere. But there's so much to do in Golden Bay over the space of a weekend, not least of which would be a walk in the Abel Tasman National Park (see page 14), accessible from the Golden Bay side at Totaranui. Also backing onto the bay is the much larger Kahurangi National Park, with its pristine forests and other attractions including walking, fishing, kayaking and caving.

If that's too much of the great outdoors, try a visit to Waikoropupu Springs, northwest of Takaka. Here the water in the southern hemisphere's largest freshwater springs bubbles up crystal clear, and can be viewed from various vantage points including walking tracks through the reserve. For a different type of watery experience, at the Bencarri Nature Park and Café you can refresh your inner person most satisfactorily — as well as hand-feed the resident long-finned eels, some of which are close to 2 metres in length and around 90 years old. In Takaka itself, the attractions of this historic settlement with its fascinating museum and excellent cafés will keep you pleasantly entertained for some time.

Northwest up State Highway 60 is the town of Collingwood, boasting two

> **There are more than 112 species of birds to be spotted on Farewell Spit.**

museums that trace the development of the district. It is also the perfect spot from which to launch yourself into a multitude of outdoor activities, one of which is an eco-tour to Farewell Spit, the northernmost point of the South Island. Administrated by the Department of Conservation, the spit is one of only three areas in New Zealand to be designated a Wetland of International Importance, a status that recognises the impressive number of birds that can be seen here — more than 112 species have been recorded!

And if you feel like stopping off between Collingwood and Takaka, try the Mussel Inn — it's not just a brewery, it also offers live entertainment, fresh mussels (well, what did you expect?) along with lots of other delectable fare, and a truly hospitable ambience. However, rumour has it that the management is allergic to mobile phones so it might pay to be discreet in your use of that technology . . . They also pay out drinks bounties on the tails of pest animals, although after paying out on 5000 possum tails, that incentive has been suspended!

North Island

Travelling Times and Distances

Each cell shows travelling time (top) and distance in km (bottom).

From \ To	Whakatane	Wellington	Wanganui	Waitomo	Waikaremoana	Thames	Tauranga	Taumarunui	Taupo	Rotorua	Palmerston North	Paihia	New Plymouth	Napier	Masterton	Kaitaia	Hicks Bay	Hamilton	Gisborne	Dargaville	Whakapapa Village	Cape Reinga	Auckland
Whangarei	7:45 / 464	12:05 / 823	9:50 / 622	6:00 / 365	10:40 / 555	4:40 / 279	6:10 / 370	7:35 / 451	6:55 / 443	6:25 / 400	10:30 / 702	1:15 / 71	9:10 / 522	9:25 / 586	12:10 / 811	3:00 / 155	11:55 / 668	4:45 / 291	11:10 / 664	1:05 / 58	8:25 / 510	5:15 / 271	3:00 / 165
Whakatane		7:55 / 545	5:10 / 358	4:05 / 235	5:40 / 241	3:40 / 209	1:35 / 97	4:15 / 257	2:45 / 165	1:25 / 85	6:20 / 424	9:00 / 534	7:00 / 384	5:15 / 308	8:00 / 533	10:55 / 618	4:10 / 205	3:05 / 193	3:25 / 201	7:50 / 478	4:15 / 262	13:00 / 734	4:55 / 298
Wellington			2:45 / 195	7:10 / 473	8:00 / 506	8:20 / 586	8:00 / 546	5:15 / 371	5:10 / 380	6:30 / 460	2:10 / 145	13:20 / 894	5:10 / 355	4:50 / 323	1:50 / 102	15:05 / 978	11:55 / 718	7:30 / 532	8:15 / 538	12:10 / 838	4:45 / 344	17:20 / 1094	9:15 / 658
Wanganui				5:10 / 273	7:00 / 435	6:55 / 479	6:35 / 439	3:15 / 171	3:05 / 229	4:25 / 309	1:10 / 74	12:05 / 693	2:25 / 160	3:50 / 252	2:50 / 183	13:50 / 777	10:40 / 643	6:05 / 331	7:15 / 467	10:55 / 637	2:45 / 141	16:05 / 894	8:00 / 457
Waitomo					7:00 / 322	3:05 / 182	2:30 / 151	1:55 / 102	2:35 / 163	2:45 / 166	6:20 / 341	7:15 / 436	3:30 / 173	5:05 / 306	8:00 / 450	9:00 / 520	8:15 / 449	1:15 / 74	7:30 / 445	6:05 / 380	2:45 / 159	11:15 / 636	3:10 / 200
Waikaremoana						6:55 / 320	5:45 / 242	6:30 / 303	4:35 / 186	4:15 / 156	5:50 / 361	11:55 / 626	10:00 / 482	3:10 / 183	6:30 / 416	13:40 / 710	6:35 / 342	5:55 / 264	2:55 / 162	10:45 / 570	6:05 / 283	15:55 / 826	7:50 / 390
Thames							2:05 / 116	4:40 / 268	3:10 / 206	2:40 / 164	6:45 / 465	5:55 / 350	6:15 / 339	5:40 / 349	8:25 / 574	7:40 / 434	7:50 / 414	1:50 / 108	7:05 / 410	4:45 / 294	4:40 / 303	15:55 / 550	1:50 / 114
Tauranga								4:05 / 235	2:25 / 156	1:30 / 86	6:00 / 415	7:25 / 441	5:40 / 308	4:55 / 299	7:40 / 524	9:10 / 525	5:45 / 302	1:55 / 106	5:00 / 298	6:15 / 385	3:45 / 236	11:25 / 641	3:20 / 205
Taumarunui									1:55 / 117	2:50 / 172	4:25 / 239	8:50 / 522	3:30 / 183	4:25 / 260	6:05 / 348	10:35 / 606	8:50 / 487	2:50 / 160	7:20 / 449	7:40 / 466	0:50 / 59	12:50 / 722	4:45 / 286
Taupo										1:20 / 80	3:35 / 259	8:10 / 514	5:25 / 296	2:30 / 143	5:15 / 368	9:55 / 598	6:55 / 370	2:10 / 152	5:25 / 332	7:00 / 458	1:30 / 97	12:10 / 714	4:05 / 278
Rotorua											4:55 / 339	7:40 / 470	5:35 / 299	3:50 / 223	6:35 / 448	9:25 / 554	5:35 / 290	1:40 / 108	4:50 / 286	6:30 / 414	2:50 / 177	11:40 / 670	3:35 / 234
Palmerston North												11:45 / 773	3:35 / 234	2:40 / 178	1:40 / 109	13:30 / 857	9:45 / 573	5:45 / 411	6:05 / 393	10:35 / 717	3:10 / 223	15:45 / 973	7:40 / 537
Paihia													10:25 / 593	10:40 / 657	13:25 / 882	2:15 / 107	13:10 / 739	6:00 / 362	12:25 / 735	2:20 / 129	9:40 / 581	4:30 / 223	4:05 / 236
New Plymouth														6:15 / 412	5:15 / 343	12:10 / 677	11:10 / 589	4:25 / 231	10:25 / 585	9:15 / 537	4:20 / 242	14:25 / 797	6:20 / 357
Napier															3:20 / 233	12:25 / 744	7:05 / 395	4:40 / 295	3:25 / 215	9:30 / 601	4:00 / 240	14:40 / 857	6:35 / 421
Masterton																15:10 / 966	10:25 / 628	7:25 / 520	6:45 / 448	12:15 / 826	4:50 / 332	17:25 / 1082	9:20 / 646
Kaitaia																	14:55 / 823	7:45 / 446	14:10 / 819	3:10 / 169	11:25 / 665	2:15 / 116	5:50 / 320
Hicks Bay																		7:15 / 398	3:40 / 180	12:00 / 683	8:25 / 467	17:10 / 939	9:05 / 503
Hamilton																			6:30 / 394	4:50 / 306	3:40 / 219	10:00 / 562	1:55 / 126
Gisborne																				11:15 / 684	6:55 / 429	16:25 / 935	8:20 / 499
Dargaville																					8:30 / 525	5:25 / 285	2:55 / 180
Whakapapa Village																						13:40 / 780	5:35 / 345
Cape Reinga																							8:05 / 436
Auckland																							

To find the distance and time needed to travel between, for example, Thames and Hicks Bay, put one finger on the name Thames and the other on the name Hicks Bay. Move sideways along the chart from Thames and upwards from Hicks Bay. Where they meet you'll see the distance between them is 414km and the travelling time is 7 hours 50 minutes. This time is for a driver travelling at 80-100 km/h on open stretches, with a small allowance for traffic delays, petrol stops and refreshments.

Times courtesy of the Ministry of Transport.

Travelling Times and Distances

To find the distance and time needed to travel between, for example, Haast and Timaru, put one finger on the name Haast and the other on the name Timaru. Move down the chart from Haast and across from Timaru. Where they meet you'll see the distance between them is 418km and the travelling time is 8 hours 10 minutes. This time is for a driver travelling at 80-100 km/h on open stretches, with a small allowance for traffic delays, petrol stops and refreshments.

Times courtesy of the Ministry of Transport.

Each cell shows travelling time (hours:minutes) above the distance (km).

	Alexandra	Blenheim	Christchurch	Collingwood	Cromwell	Dunedin	Franz Josef	Geraldine	Gore	Greymouth	Haast	Invercargill	Kaikoura	Milford Sound	Aoraki/Mount Cook	Murchison	Nelson	Oamaru	Picton	Queenstown	Te Anau	Tekapo	Timaru	Twizel	Wanaka
Blenheim	11:10 / 786																								
Christchurch	6:40 / 455	4:35 / 308																							
Collingwood	16:45 / 964	4:10 / 251	7:50 / 509																						
Cromwell	0:35 / 31	10:55 / 733	6:20 / 410	16:05 / 939																					
Dunedin	3:00 / 190	9:35 / 670	5:00 / 362	12:50 / 871	3:35 / 221																				
Franz Josef	7:45 / 373	8:15 / 486	6:25 / 395	9:20 / 582	6:45 / 342	12:10 / 563																			
Geraldine	5:15 / 315	6:25 / 446	1:50 / 138	9:40 / 697	4:30 / 273	3:25 / 232	7:45 / 481																		
Gore	2:00 / 136	11:50 / 821	7:15 / 513	15:05 / 1022	2:35 / 167	2:15 / 151	7:05 / 509	5:40 / 387																	
Greymouth	9:50 / 661	5:05 / 324	4:10 / 258	6:10 / 384	9:55 / 526	8:10 / 551	3:10 / 177	5:15 / 329	10:25 / 704																
Haast	5:10 / 231	10:45 / 634	8:55 / 535	11:55 / 720	4:15 / 200	9:35 / 421	2:20 / 148	8:10 / 431	6:45 / 367	5:40 / 317															
Invercargill	2:55 / 202	12:45 / 887	8:10 / 579	16:00 / 1088	3:30 / 233	3:10 / 217	10:45 / 575	6:35 / 449	0:55 / 66	11:20 / 769	8:10 / 433														
Kaikoura	9:20 / 657	1:50 / 129	2:50 / 183	6:00 / 380	9:10 / 607	7:50 / 545	8:55 / 550	4:40 / 321	9:05 / 696	7:00 / 338	11:25 / 710	11:00 / 762													
Milford Sound	6:20 / 370	15:15 / 1081	11:35 / 773	21:55 / 1232	6:00 / 336	6:35 / 411	12:40 / 678	9:45 / 635	4:20 / 260	16:00 / 860	10:15 / 539	4:45 / 278	16:15 / 956												
Aoraki/Mount Cook	3:30 / 242	9:30 / 639	4:55 / 331	12:45 / 840	3:55 / 201	4:35 / 331	9:00 / 498	2:55 / 187	5:30 / 378	8:55 / 510	6:25 / 356	7:50 / 444	7:45 / 514	8:55 / 550											
Murchison	13:30 / 734	2:30 / 153	4:15 / 292	3:35 / 219	12:35 / 693	9:15 / 654	5:45 / 340	6:10 / 430	11:30 / 842	2:35 / 167	8:20 / 503	12:25 / 871	5:10 / 299	16:35 / 1029	9:00 / 623										
Nelson	12:55 / 865	1:45 / 116	6:15 / 424	1:45 / 135	12:35 / 845	11:05 / 786	7:45 / 469	8:05 / 562	13:30 / 937	4:35 / 290	10:15 / 609	14:15 / 1003	3:35 / 245	18:35 / 1146	10:30 / 755	2:00 / 129									
Oamaru	3:20 / 223	7:55 / 555	3:20 / 247	11:20 / 756	3:30 / 228	1:40 / 115	9:25 / 506	1:45 / 123	3:55 / 266	7:30 / 443	7:00 / 376	4:50 / 332	6:10 / 430	8:15 / 526	3:55 / 216	7:35 / 539	9:35 / 671								
Picton	11:40 / 791	0:25 / 28	5:00 / 336	4:20 / 245	11:20 / 761	10:00 / 698	8:40 / 531	6:55 / 474	12:15 / 849	5:30 / 352	11:10 / 671	13:10 / 915	2:15 / 157	18:25 / 1108	9:45 / 687	2:55 / 191	2:10 / 110	8:20 / 583							
Queenstown	1:30 / 93	11:50 / 794	7:15 / 486	17:05 / 961	0:55 / 62	4:25 / 283	7:45 / 404	6:10 / 346	2:35 / 169	10:55 / 583	5:10 / 262	3:00 / 187	11:10 / 669	5:05 / 291	3:50 / 263	11:30 / 775	13:30 / 910	4:50 / 319	13:20 / 822						
Te Anau	4:00 / 249	13:50 / 960	9:15 / 652	19:50 / 1117	3:40 / 217	4:15 / 290	10:30 / 560	7:25 / 516	2:00 / 139	13:40 / 739	7:55 / 418	2:25 / 152	13:55 / 835	2:20 / 121	6:30 / 429	14:15 / 944	16:15 / 1025	5:55 / 404	16:05 / 988	2:45 / 170					
Tekapo	3:35 / 227	7:55 / 534	3:20 / 226	11:10 / 785	3:00 / 196	4:30 / 303	9:15 / 485	1:30 / 88	5:35 / 363	6:00 / 417	6:40 / 343	6:55 / 429	6:10 / 409	9:00 / 532	1:25 / 99	7:25 / 518	9:35 / 650	2:50 / 188	8:25 / 562	5:00 / 258	6:40 / 428				
Timaru	4:40 / 307	6:45 / 471	2:10 / 163	10:00 / 672	4:25 / 268	2:50 / 199	10:45 / 493	0:35 / 35	5:05 / 350	5:20 / 352	8:10 / 418	6:00 / 416	5:20 / 346	9:25 / 610	3:10 / 203	6:25 / 455	8:25 / 587	1:10 / 84	7:10 / 499	5:35 / 335	7:05 / 489	1:40 / 104			
Twizel	2:40 / 169	8:50 / 592	4:15 / 284	12:05 / 843	2:05 / 138	3:45 / 261	7:30 / 427	2:25 / 146	4:40 / 316	6:55 / 475	5:35 / 285	6:00 / 371	7:05 / 467	8:05 / 474	0:50 / 63	8:20 / 576	10:30 / 708	2:05 / 146	9:15 / 620	3:00 / 200	5:45 / 370	0:55 / 58	2:35 / 162		
Wanaka	1:25 / 86	11:20 / 745	6:30 / 424	15:10 / 839	0:50 / 55	4:25 / 276	5:55 / 287	5:25 / 286	3:25 / 222	9:05 / 469	3:20 / 145	4:40 / 285	9:20 / 607	6:55 / 394	3:00 / 203	10:45 / 715	12:45 / 848	3:40 / 231	11:45 / 773	1:50 / 117	4:35 / 273	3:20 / 198	4:35 / 273	2:15 / 140	
Westport	11:35 / 761	4:15 / 264	5:10 / 333	5:20 / 320	11:45 / 639	10:55 / 695	4:55 / 277	7:45 / 432	12:10 / 804	1:45 / 101	7:30 / 437	13:05 / 869	5:30 / 340	16:05 / 951	10:00 / 664	1:45 / 101	3:45 / 226	8:30 / 580	4:40 / 288	12:30 / 664	14:30 / 830	14:10 / 559	8:05 / 497	9:25 / 617	10:45 / 558

Index of activities by region

Image Credits

Alpine Pacific Tourism: 134, 135, 143, 214
Bay of Islands Country Rock Festival (Donna Russell): 198, 199
Beach Hop Central (Noddy Watts): 180, 181
Brandish Advertising: 67
Bookabach: 61 (b)
Caleta Streetrace: 66
Cellar Door (Kendra Johnson): 168, 169
Christchurch and Canterbury Tourism: 70, 121, 131, 140
Destination Fiordland: 44 (Rod Willett), 45 (Rob Suisted), 64 (b), 88, 89 (Sue Lovell), 118 (Graham Dainty), 119 (Graham Dainty), cover left
Destination Manawatu: 220, 221
Destination Marlborough: 95, 104, 105 (b), 164, 165, back cover top
Destination Northland: 14, 15, 30, 31, 92, 93, 108, 109, 126, 130 (l), 148, 149, 152, 154, back cover second from top, back cover second from bottom
Destination Rotorua: 10, 22, 23, 71, 74, 128, 142, 143, 206
Eco-fest: 162, 163
Food Hawke's Bay: 156
Gate Photography, Tauranga: 186, 187
Hamilton Regional Tourism: 63, 64 (t), 65, 72, 73, cover second from left
Hawke's Bay Incorporated: 20, 21, 50, 130 (r), 150, 153, cover right
Interislander: 99
Jonathan Cowie: 126
Marlborough Wine Festival: 190, 191 (Frank Gasteiger)
Photo New Zealand: 18 (Arno Gasteiger), 28 (Arno Gasteiger), 29 (Colin Monteath, Hedgehog House), 36 (Stephen Goodenough), 38 (Rob Brown), 39 (Stephen Goodenough), 40 (Stephen Goodenough), 41 (Pat Barrett, Hedgehog House), 49 (t, Matheson Beaumont), 53 (b, Arno Gasteiger), 60 (Kim Christensen), 61 (t, Mike Langford), 62 (Gerhard Egger), 68, 69 (Colin Monteath, Hedgehog House), 74 (Gerhard Egger), 76 (Nick Servian), 77 (Tony Stewart), 79 (Gerhard Egger), 82 (Arno Gasteiger), 91 (Roy Sinclair, Hedgehog House), 94 (Wendy Cain), 97 (Rob Brown), 98 (Graeme Matthews), 105 (Arno Gasteiger), 106

(Rob Brown), 110 (Rob Brown, Hedgehog House), 111 (Craig Macintosh), 112, 114, 117 (Kim Christensen), 124 (Chris McLennan), 125 (Chris McLennan), 132 (Geoff Mason), 133 (Arno Gasteiger), 136 (Chris McLennan, Hedgehog House), 137 (Colin Monteath, Hedgehog House),138 (Ian Trafford), 139 (Ian Stirling, Hedgehog House), 141 (Lloyd Park),144 (Nick Servian), 145 (Ian Trafford), 155 (Arno Gasteiger), 161 (Forrest Smyth), 166 (Tim Cuff), 167 (Julia Thorne), 170 (Andy Radka), 172 (Tony Stewart), 173 (John Doogan), 174 (Ian Trafford), 175 (Ian Trafford), 185 (Paul Stieller), 194 (Julia Thorne), 200 (Andy Radka), 201 (Nick Servian), 202 (Ian Batchelor), 207 (Kim Christensen), 215 (Arno Gasteiger), 216 (John Rendle, Hedgehog House), 217 (Mead Norton), 218 (Ian Trafford), 226 (Lynette Mill), 229 (Mike Langford), 230 (Darryl Torkler), 231 (Ian Trafford), cover main pic (Arno Gasteiger)
Positively Wellington Tourism: 26, 32, 33, 53 (t)
Sarah Ell: 13 (b), 19, 24, 78, 210, 211, 212, 213, back cover bottom
Stewart Island Experience/Real Journeys: 100, 101 (r), cover second from right
Supersport Images: 183
Tongariro National Trout Centre Society: 58, 59 (Peter Sutcliffe)
Tourism Auckland: 56 (l), 80, 81, 113, 116, 122, 146
Tourism Central Otago: 25, 34, 35, 54, 127, 160, 222, 223, 228, back cover middle
Tourism Coromandel (Andy Belcher): 16, 59, 86, 87, 227
Tourism Dunedin: 27, 48, 49 (b), 147, 158, 192, 193
Tourism Eastland: 12, 13 (t)
Tranz Scenic: 82, 90
Venture Southland: 96, 101 (l), 189
Venture Taranaki: 56 (r), 58, 123, 176, 177, 204, 205, 208, 209, 224, 225
Visit Oamaru: 47 (r), 196, 197
Visit Ruapehu: 42, 43, 46, 47 (l), 85
Waiheke Olive Festival (Denis la Touche): 195
Wanganui District Council: 84, 115
Whakatane District Council: 51, 102, 103, 120
Whitestone Cheese Rolling (Yannick Joris): 179

Useful websites

www.aatravel.co.nz — One of New Zealand's most comprehensive and user-friendly travel websites — an excellent planning tool for Kiwis wanting to plan their next must-do weekend away
www.doc.govt.nz — Information on parks, tracks and huts

Regional tourism information

Alpine Pacific Triangle: www.hurunui.com
Auckland: www.aucklandnz.com
Bay of Plenty: www.bayofplentynz.com
Central Otago: www.centralotagonz.com
Central South Island: www.southisland.org.nz
Christchurch and Canterbury: www.christchurchnz.com
Coromandel: www.thecoromandel.com
Dunedin: www.dunedinnz.com
Eastland: www.gisbornenz.com
Fiordland: www.fiordland.org.nz
Hawke's Bay: www.hawkesbaynz.com
Kapiti– Horowhenua: www.naturecoast.co.nz
Lake Taupo: www.laketauponz.com
Lake Wanaka Tourism: www.lakewanaka.co.nz
Manawatu: www.manawatunz.co.nz

Marlborough: www.destinationmarlborough.com
Mt Cook Mackenzie: www.mtcooknz.com
Nelson– Tasman: www.nelsonnz.com
Northland: www.northlandnz.com
Queenstown: www.queenstown-nz.co.nz
Rotorua: www.rotoruanz.com
Ruapehu: www.visitruapehu.com
Southland: www.southland.org.nz
Taranaki: www.taranaki.co.nz
Waikato: www.waikatonz.co.nz
Wairarapa: www.wairarapanz.com
Waitaki: www.visitoamaru.co.nz
Wanganui: www.wanganui.com
Wellington: www.wellingtonnz.com
West Coast: www.west-coast.co.nz

Index